hidden heroes

MISTI BURMEISTER

synergy
sp press

Synergy Press books may be purchased in bulk for educational, business,
or sales promotional use. For information please write:
order@synergypressonline.com

FIRST EDITION

Designed by Jennifer Tyson

Library of Congress Cataloging-in-Publishing Data

Burmeister, Misti L.
    Hidden Heroes
Personal Leadership / Misti Burmeister. – 1st ed.
        p. cm.
    Includes references.
    ISBN: 978-0-9802209-3-3
1. Burmeister, Misti, date.
2. Women-United States-Biography.
3. Young Women-United States-Biography.
4. Young Entrepreneurs-United States-Biography.
5. Heroes. I. Title

dedication

I am dedicating this book to two of the most funny (albeit,
a *lil* redneck), courageous, kind, resourceful, loving people I know:
my parents, Eileen and Jim Burmeister — two heroes who are no longer
hidden from my sight. First, thank you for putting up with me!
Second, thank you for teaching me to take myself a *lot* less seriously
and to enjoy my life regardless of my successes, or lack thereof.
Finally, thank you for standing by my side throughout it *all* and instilling
within me the courage to take this journey. I love you more than you
can imagine and I'm immensely grateful to have *you* as my parents.

contents

Introduction
Hero with My Face (plus yours and a thousand of our friends) IX

The Hero's Journey, Stage 1
Obstacles and Overcoming Self 3

TRANSFORMATION: *From Judgement to Forgiveness* 4
The Lesson of Fierce Kindness 4
Pandora's Box 7

TRANSFORMATION: *From Fear to Freedom* 9
Sleepless Nights and Answered Prayers 10
Compassion for the Liar: Facing the Truth Within 18
Warts and All: An Unlikely Mirror 21
INTERLUDE: *"Starbursts"* 28

The Hero's Journey, Stage 2
Guides Along the Way 29

TRANSFORMATION: *From Insecurity to Self-Esteem* 30
Fight or Flight 31
Carburetor Confidence 33

TRANSFORMATION: *From Being Seen to Seeing* 36
Are the Fish Jumping? 36
The Transformation of Compassion: A Shift in Perspective 39
Mirror, Mirror on the Wall 41

TRANSFORMATION: *From Isolation to Friendship* 43
Zig Ziglar and the Cure for Loneliness 45
Jasmine: The Poetry of Friendship 48
INTERLUDE: *"Bare"* 53

The Hero's Journey, Stage 3
Self-Knowledge Beneath the Surface 55

TRANSFORMATION: *From Outward Success to Inner Security* 56
Hidden Treasure in Bali 57
Seek Peace and Pursue It 63
Embracing the Mystery of Not Knowing 66
INTERLUDE: *"Lifted"* 70

The Hero's Journey, Stage 4
Living In and Giving Back to the World — a Boon 71

TRANSFORMATION: *From Fiasco to Fierce Kindness* 72
Odyssey 74
A Tale of Two Mentors 77
College Algebra 80
Coming Out and Coming Home 82
Writing as a Path to Compassion 86
INTERLUDE: *"Let Go of the Trying"* 90

The Hero's Journey, Stage 5
Heroes, Heroes Everywhere! 91

TRANSFORMATION: *From Ordinary People to Heroes* 92
Everyday Heroes 92
Diane: My Sister, My Hero 94
A Heroic Inheritance: 'Tis Easier to Give Than to Receive 98
Craig: Learning to Trust in the Unseen 99
Principal Wiser 102
Danny: The Gift of Grace 105
Francesca: The Secret Superhero Identity of My Partner 107
INTERLUDE: *"Releasing my Prisoner"* 112

ONGOING TRANSFORMATION: *Manifesting the Hero Within* 113
Finding Calm in the Storm 113
Wholeness Is a Balancing Act: A Hero with Two Faces 115

NOTES 122

"We have not even to risk the adventure alone, for the heroes of all time have gone before us — the labyrinth is thoroughly known. We have only to follow the thread of the hero's path, and where we had thought to find an abomination, we shall find a god; where we had thought to slay another, we shall slay ourselves; where we had thought to travel outward, we shall come to the center of our own existence. And where we had thought to be alone, we shall be with all the world."

JOSEPH CAMPBELL
The Hero With A Thousand Faces

introduction

HERO WITH MY FACE
(plus yours and a thousand of our friends)

Have you ever wanted so desperately to know where you fit into this world? Have you ever wanted to know that who you are matters and that all you've done has added value to humankind – and to the lives of those around you? Have you ever wanted someone to take your hand and show you the way, to guide you to your greatness? Have you ever felt so isolated and alone that no matter how many people were around you at any particular time, you wanted to scream, "Here I am! Can you see me?"

I have … over and over, for as long I can remember. These questions are at the heart of the issues I've struggled with throughout my life. But it wasn't until I began writing this book that I put it all together. Throughout this journey, as I shared my stories with others, I realized something powerful – I am not the only one who's ever felt this way. I found the more authentic my struggles and my breakthroughs, the more vulnerable or "embarrassing" the information I shared, the more others related. I hope the same is true for you, because, chances are, you are on your own journey – and the road is easier when you know you're not alone.

The book you are about to read is not the one I intended to write. I started it the week after "Be a Part of the Solution," an event I hosted to bring together top entrepreneurs in the D.C. area to share strategies for success. My poet friend, Jasmine, and I loaded up the car and headed to the beach to write and be inspired together, a tradition that has strengthened both our writing and our friendship over the years. The trip was perfectly timed. My head and laptop were full of the information I needed for the book I was writing for young professionals, and I was set to return with a complete manuscript.

Excited to write, I jumped out of bed the first morning, threw on my sweater and headed downstairs. I thought I'd warm up by pounding out a story or two, which would ultimately relate to the young professionals book. Three hours later, as Jasmine was just getting out of bed, I stopped to read what I had written — not one word of which was about young professionals struggling to find their place in the workforce.

Instead, I had written a response to what one of the "Be a Part of the Solution" panelists said about heroes. Doug, an incredible entrepreneur, humanitarian and person, talked about how important role models have been in his life, so much so that he prints bios of people who inspire him and keeps them close by at all times. As I listened to him talk about how his heroes have shaped his success, I was inspired. As I wrote that first morning, I realized a seismic shift had taken place in my understanding of heroes, a shift that has changed my life.

Initially, I missed the significance and was caught off guard and off task. Disappointed, I said, "Jasmine, I have just wasted three precious hours of writing time." Then, I proceeded to read her the words I hadn't meant to write.

When I finished, she said, "I have chills, Misti. That's powerful stuff."

"Yes, it's powerful," I said, still irritated — and still not getting it. "But it doesn't relate to the book I'm focused on right *now*."

As the words came out of my mouth, a wave of truth washed over me. Suddenly, the furthest thing from my mind and heart was generational dynamics in the workplace. But this book was already halfway written. I knew it would help others *and* add to my credibility. And if I put it on hold to write a book about heroes, the information could become outdated.

When I returned to my computer 30 minutes later, determined to focus on young pros, I couldn't open the document. Instead, I felt this incessant pull to continue writing where I'd left off. That day, I decided to give up control, and, instead, allow my writing to chart its own course, to flow through me as *it* saw fit. As I delved more deeply, I decided my new book would be about reframing the idea of heroes. I would figure out who my heroes are: the authors, speakers and famous people who inspire me and whose influence has molded my life and philosophies.

However, after more writing and deeper epiphanies, I realized this book has more to do with discovering the heroes around me – the everyday people in my past and present who, though utterly human and therefore utterly flawed, have impacted my life in major ways.

The idea of a "hero" is not a new one. Sure, there's Superman and company, but I'm talking about people whose heroism depends on being fully and thoroughly human. We use the word all the time to refer to people who have accomplished something, created something or lived in a way that changes how we think and feel about the world and opens our minds to new perspectives. Often these heroes are familiar faces: the firefighter who went back in to save the family parakeet, the elementary school teacher who told us we could write, the coach who inspired us to push to the next level of excellence or the parent who showed up at every important school event. What these people have in common is that they transform the way we see ourselves and the world. Through their everyday heroics, they show us that we also have it in us to achieve the impossible, to unveil the hero within.

And then a truly amazing transformation began. When I started looking for the heroism in them, I began looking at myself a little more compassionately. That changed everything – not only the scope of the book,

but also *me*. Instead of a story of philosophy and inspiration, this book became a journey, one that led me back into my past – and into some memories so painful that I'd blocked or ignored them for years.

Heroism is not just about accomplishments. Before embarking on this
journey, I had my fair share of achievements. By outward standards, I was
"a success." I published a book, *From Boomers to Bloggers*, which made
the *Washington Post's* best seller list, among others. I founded my own
company, Inspirion LLC, and embarked on a flourishing career helping
companies leverage generational differences. I was well-traveled, well-read
and well-supported, but I still had not yet discovered the hero within.

In his book, *The Hero with a Thousand Faces*, Joseph Campbell describes
the hero's journey as one that we are all invited to take. He shows us that
in all good stories, and in our own ordinary lives, it is when an individual must embark on a journey – when she must face pain and hope, acceptance and release, confusion and understanding – that growth happens
and a hero is born. Adapting Campbell's stages as a guide (and as section
headings of this book), I opened up wounds and fought for forgiveness.

No individual who embarks on such a journey remains unchanged. The
transformation is simultaneously painful, scary, wonderful and inspiring.
Before writing this book, many of my memories seemed too difficult to
face. But as I wrote, the difficulty melted and the gifts shone through. I
have come to see the heroes who surrounded me throughout my life, who
have played a role in my journey. Slowly, I began seeing how these people and my life's stories helped me become the woman I am today, and
how I carry them with me as I continue forward. I began the process of
unveiling the hero in me – the core of who I am, without all the titles
and big successes I've relied on to hold me up.

Writing this book has helped me to meet and fall in love with the soul
I have always been – and the woman I am constantly becoming. I am
noticing and listening to myself more intently – and writing through it.
I'm learning to appreciate what's there, without labeling myself or my past

actions as "right" or "wrong." And in exposing myself and my insecurities, I'm healing.

"There's no need to explore your past, Misti," many said along the way. "Just start right here where you are. Just live your life from this moment and forget the rest." Yes, I believe being present to our lives and ourselves is important and healthy. But our pasts are part of who we are, and knowing ourselves is worth the reflection, as painful as it may be. After all, those who forget their histories are doomed to repeat them, right?

Writing this book took me on a hero's journey – a journey I welcome you to take with me. Throughout the book, you will notice "Try This" questions. These are the reflections that have led me to wholeness. Consider taking the time to journal or just jot down your thoughts about the questions that hit home for you. I hope they lead you to your own truths.

While I have uncovered and rediscovered myself through this book, I know the journey of coming to know ourselves lasts as long as we breathe. This book is a part of my own quest for peace and freedom. And though the change begins within, it reverberates throughout the world. The transformation I have experienced on this journey has affected the way I see and relate to others. It is amazing how compassion toward oneself manifests into compassion toward others. And from that tiny shift in attitude, everyone is transformed. I now see heroes everywhere – all around and *inside* me.

By taking the time to hear ourselves, share our struggles and breakthroughs, and listen, really listen, to others' stories, we create a space for each of us to see and discover the hero *within*.

MISTI BURMEISTER
May 24, 2011

stage one
Obstacles and Overcoming Self

TRANSFORMATION:
From Judgement to Forgiveness

"A grownup is a child with layers on."
WOODY HARRELSON

This is the journey from judgment to, ultimately, forgiveness – but not in the traditional sense. I no longer think of forgiveness as something that we give. Instead, I define forgiveness by what we get: the opportunity to be able to say, with authenticity, "Thank you for giving me that experience." As it turns out, forgiveness begins right here, with us. We have to thank ourselves for the experiences we put ourselves through – good, bad or indifferent. Finding forgiveness for oneself is the only way to authentic forgiveness of others; yet, it may not be easy to give at first. Appreciating ourselves for the experiences that have created havoc and turmoil inside of us seems, at first, like lunacy. As it turns out, we're all a little crazy anyway (you know, unique and special, just like everyone else), so venture forth anyway!

> **try this:**
> *Imagine that you are taking the journey in search of reconciliation with your past, or your shadow side. What is your shadow side? What are the memories, self-defeating thoughts, pain and secrets weighing you down? Journal about your fears and how you arm/protect yourself.*

THE LESSON OF FIERCE KINDNESS

⚜

Socrates says that all knowledge is a process of remembering, that we are born knowing everything and through the distraction of life, we forget everything, starting with ourselves. Regaining wisdom requires unflinching, yet compassionate, self-examination. The task of remembering some of our most embarrassing and painful moments is not an easy one. Often, it is difficult to see how the remembering will lead to wholeness and wisdom. That's where compassion comes in.

One evening, as I prepared to meditate, it hit me like a tsunami as it crashes against land, destroying buildings, moving cars, and killing or displacing people. Images of myself as a little girl having sex with random boys overwhelmed my mind, and all I could think was, "I'm disgusting. I make bad choices for myself. I'm worthless." I wasn't sure whether I should fall to my knees, curl up into a little ball, cry and resist the feelings, or just ride the wave.

Of course, I would have rather have found something more fun to distract myself – pizza, chocolate, work, a root canal ... anything. But I knew that if I didn't go through this now, I'd be dealing with it until I did.

Thank God I was not home alone. My partner, Francesca, was downstairs watching television. With blurry vision, I stumbled half-way down the stairs, crumbled on the ground and began wailing.

Francesca quickly made her way over to me. "What is it, Misti?" she asked.

I tried to answer but my words were hardly coherent, and my body began convulsing with sobs, thrusting forward as if trying to release its torment. Fortunately, Francesca's tight grip kept me from tumbling the rest of the way down the stairs.

I didn't yet know how to express what was wrong, but after a few minutes I was at least able to mumble something about seeing myself for the first time. She held; I cried. Eventually, I calmed down enough to share my thoughts. "That little girl is me, Francesca," I sobbed. "She's me."

I told her some of the memories that had just surfaced – how I could see myself doing dangerous, self-destructive things, and more importantly, could hear again that inner voice of judgment and criticism that had begun the moment I performed such acts. These were shadows from my past, memories I had blocked long ago, so I had never experienced or spoken of them as if they had actually happened to *me*. "I did those things to myself," I yelled. "And I hated myself for it." Her grip grew stronger as my sobs and convulsions grew more violent.

After several minutes, I calmed down enough to make a decision. "I love her, Francesca," I said firmly. "I love me. I needed to feel loved and visible, and those sexual acts were all I knew at the time." The sobs began again. "It's all I knew!"

I collapsed backward onto the stairs, turned on my left side and held myself for a few minutes. Though I knew Francesca's knees were tiring from kneeling on the stairs (and the large stack of used tissues beside us indicated we'd been there a while), she stayed with me for several more minutes. Eventually, those images softened with compassion for myself, which was held by Francesca's love.

While I imagine that experience was horrifying for Francesca, I am for-ever grateful for her fierce kindness. She knew I needed to go through what-ever I was experiencing. She didn't push for answers, though I know it was hard for her to wait for them, and hearing an explanation would have made the whole thing easier for her. Instead, she listened and let me express as I needed to in that moment. And we never needed to talk about it again. That's the beauty of our friendship – that nothing more needed to be said. She understood I was on a journey and that I simply needed her support.

Francesca's grip was the kindness I needed to penetrate the scars I'd just opened around my heart. It allowed me to look at myself with kindness rather than self-hatred for my "bad" decisions, freeing me to love myself on a new level.

On the journey to wholeness and freedom, having a strong support sys-tem makes it feel safer to be vulnerable – to release the fear and the pro-tective layers and to stand naked before the truth. I've known that nakedness and the freedom it provides. It's not always comfortable. But it is always worth it.

PANDORA'S BOX

❧

I was 11 years old, living in Commerce City, Colorado, stealing, fighting, knowingly breaking the law by climbing on top of the school building (wondering whether I could withstand the impact if I jumped), and randomly having sex with boys.

I don't remember all of my sexual partners growing up, but there is one incident I can vividly recall. In the center of my brother's long, narrow basement room, there was a pool table. His bed was on one side of it, and a couch was on the other. While my brother played video games on the couch, I had sex with one of his friends on his bed. I barely remember what it felt like physically, but I remember hoping it would end soon.

Once he was done, I wrapped a sheet around my body and rushed out of my brother's room across the small hallway into my 15-year-old sister's room to show her what I had just done. She was sexually active, so I thought she'd be impressed, that it would somehow get her to like me.

The next words out of her mouth let me know that seeing her little sister wrapped up in a sheet after having sex with a guy she barely knew wasn't as appealing (or as impressive) as I had hoped. Who would have guessed?

She was appalled and disgusted. My mind went hazy and my heart began to panic. If not for acceptance, love and closeness, I wouldn't have done this. What went wrong? How could I have let some strange guy use my body for pleasure if I wasn't getting anything out of it? Could anyone see my hurt? Could I even see it myself? Not then.

What I remember most from this time in my life was my extreme need to be seen. I did everything I could to gain attention, even if, in the end, it was destructive. So, I understand why people do outlandish or socially unacceptable things; it's their way of dealing with loneliness and isolation.

Experiences that are too difficult for someone with no earthly idea how to deal with the emotions that follow are common. Young people cut themselves to deal with the pain of not being seen and acknowledged.

They give themselves away sexually and emotionally, often long before they're truly ready for such risks. And many people just remain silent and hope their fears, pain and haunting memories will magically go away. This purposeful ignorance is not a conscious or malicious decision; rather, it is our subconscious way of coping with "too much" and not having the resources to accept what has happened, embrace it and move forward.

Are there other options for moving past the most difficult events in our lives? Yes, and for me, it started with being brave enough to stand naked before myself, to open my eyes to my stories and process them with unconditional love. Twenty years later, I can usually look back at this time in my life with a great sense of compassion for the little girl who knew no other way. But I have not always been able to think of my inner child with the love, kindness and forgiveness necessary to heal the woman with the painful past.

This journey has required me to relive memories I'd blocked, to open wounds I thought had healed. Instead, I had only neglected them to the point that they grew infected, and though they closed, they never *healed* at all. Sure, I could talk about some of the experiences I share in this book, but I never experienced these stories as if they were *mine*. When I finally opened Pandora's Box, allowing all the perceived horrors of my life to surface, I didn't find chaos and destruction. I found freedom, more than I'd ever known. The initial shock of releasing the truth was immensely painful, but as I continue to face those truths with forgiveness and kindness in my heart, I feel weightless.

Those experiences, however difficult, helped make me who I am today, or rather, *surviving*

> try this:
>
> *Remember yourself as a child and imagine that child alive within you. Speak to this younger version of yourself, or write a letter. What do you wish you could say or do for this child? What does he/she need to survive and thrive? What is most comforting to this child?*

them and finally acknowledging that they happened without judging myself, has strengthened my spirit. To reject them is akin to rejecting part of who I am. Each experience I'm reliving (and subsequently *releasing*) is helping to guide me back to my authentic self – the one beneath the layers of self-doubt, self-criticism and destructive tendencies.

And, as with most struggles in my life, I get by with a little help from my friends. When I need to get out of my head and back into my heart, there is usually at least one person in my life who will take the time to listen, to alleviate my feeling of isolation and help me calm my little girl so I can feel safe again. When I can't get anyone on the phone, despite pushing redial 15 times, I make do with strangers. I head to the store and do goofy things to make people laugh or offer them kind words. Just short exchanges like: "You're beautiful." "I love your smile." "Does my underwear look good with this outfit?" (Note: You gotta find the right person for that last one!)

With support and kind words, even when I must give these to myself, I can find my way back to a quiet, calm place, where I can look at myself with compassion once again, hear my own voice and allow my authentic self to guide me back onto that hero's path.

TRANSFORMATION:
From Fear to Freedom

"Fear can be a great motivator, but not necessarily
a healthy one. We are all afraid of something.
But what happens when we let go of the fear?"

ELISABETH KÜBLER-ROSS

Fear can be a great motivator, but not necessarily a healthy one. We are all afraid of something. But what happens when we let go of the fear?

This was a question that plagued me for some time: Who and where would I be if I was not afraid and anxious much of the time? In fact, it was one of my success secrets, driving me to frantically send out dozens of e-mails whenever I had a chance, attend as many networking functions as possible, spend the day on the phone and stay up late in the night keeping myself busy doing anything that would get me seen, get me heard and somehow show me my way to success.

I came to rely on that fear, and held tightly to it, like people who stay in abusive relationships, because after all, it's the devil that you know. Letting go of fear is terrifying, but while it's still with me much of the time, I can see it better now, acknowledge it, recognize it for what it is and make kinder choices for myself. Heroes can be afraid without diminishing their bravery, because they don't let it paralyze them. It's the same for the hero within.

"We are all more than we know," writes Rachel Naomi Remen. "Integrity rarely means we need to add something to ourselves: it is more an undoing than a doing, a freeing ourselves from beliefs we have about who we are." For me, letting go of anxiety takes consistently undoing. It also requires accepting the help of professionals and medication, an acquiescence that made me look hard at who I am beneath the fear. But as usual, doing so led me to deeper truths, calming my anxiety and helping me to recognize my unhealthy patterns.

SLEEPLESS NIGHTS AND
ANSWERED PRAYERS

When I was a child, my anxiety manifested in bed wetting. Being sent home from school for smelling like dried pee was not the most pleasant experience for an early teenager. In terms of things you hope to never experience, it probably ranks right up there with jury duty and being kicked repeatedly with a golf shoe. Despite the torment from my classmates and siblings, who affectionately referred to me as "Misti-pissty," I could not stop wetting the bed. In hindsight, it probably would have helped matters if I had bathed before going to school – but hey, you live, you learn.

At the time, I figured I wet the bed because I was lazy or had an exceptionally small bladder, which would need to be corrected at some point. Choosing to believe I was not just *that* lazy, I decided it must be the latter.

When I was 12 years old, my bedwetting became what felt like a life-or-death situation. Sharing a room with my sister, Diane, who is three and a half years my senior, was exciting and terrifying. I loved the idea of hanging out with her; she was cool. But sharing space with her lost some of its appeal when I began fearing for my life. Either she had a very sensitive nose, or the smell of dried urine was truly capable of causing a gag reflex. I tried to hide the smell by piling towels and extra sheets on top of the incriminating evidence, but she always knew.

By early evening, when it was time to retreat to our rooms and settle in, our usual exchange went something like this: "You disgusting ___. You wet your bed again, didn't you Misti-pissty? You're nasty. Get away from me." Siblings can be so pleasant to one another.

I made a pact with myself to stop wetting the bed. I had absolutely no idea *how*, but the situation was dire. I had tried cutting off liquid intake two hours before bed for years, and it had never worked. But I was recommitted (and terrified of Diane), and eventually, I developed a strategy that worked. It involved talking myself into getting up in the middle of the night and stumbling to the bathroom. If worse came to worse, I immediately stripped my bed and washed the sheets, which at least let her know I was trying.

While my sister's wrath cured me of a bad habit or two over the years, it did little to help my chronic anxiety. As a young adult, insomnia became the major symptom.

Until my late teens, I slept about 12 hours a night, but then everything changed. For no obvious reason, it suddenly became hard for me to fall asleep, and once I did finally drift off, I often woke up in the middle of the night, my heart beating a million miles a minute, unable to get back to sleep.

Two weeks of this was enough to make me feel crazy, so I set an appointment with my general practitioner, who prescribed antidepressants. I tried those for a couple weeks. No success.

Before long, I found myself obsessing about sleep. I tried watching television to relax, reading a book and just lying in bed waiting to get tired enough to sleep. But the problem escalated quickly, and I soon found myself unable to sleep for weeks on end.

During the day, I was so exhausted and irritable that I could hardly wait for bedtime. But at night, the noises I'd always slept through became magnified and unbearable. The sound of passing trains 200 yards from our home, the loud voices of my family members, the crop dusters in the morning, my parents using the bathroom (which happened to be right next to my room) and my father's insistence on using his power tools right outside my bedroom window – these sounds were no longer background noise or minor annoyances; they were deafening and debilitating. Of course, the voices in my head obsessing about not sleeping were the greatest source of noise.

My doctor sent me to a neurologist, who prescribed different meds, but nothing helped. Feeling as though I had exhausted my options, I tried to control every part of my environment. I can only imagine how annoying I was to live with, as I began making unreasonable requests for silence. Fights over noise became part of our family evening routine and the sleepless nights continued. But no matter how quiet my family was, I didn't sleep, so I began looking for a room to rent.

My two new roommates understood my sleeping issues and often tiptoed upstairs at night to ensure they didn't wake me. I was grateful for their thoughtfulness, but their silence didn't fix the problem. I often went a week or more without sleep, crashed for six or seven hours and then started the painful cycle again. I thought I would go crazy (if it wasn't already too late for that) and wondered whether I could die from lack of sleep.

I became obsessed over my nightly routine. Unknowingly, I programmed my subconscious mind to worry about my environment in the evenings, and of course, worry is not conducive to slumber. Over the next decade, I learned to get by on very little sleep. Though I became accustomed to it, I also longed for the days when I could easily snooze for 12 to 14 hours at a time.

Just over three years ago I began seeing a therapist named Amy, a licensed hypnotist and EMDR (eye movement desensitization response) specialist. Conventional medicine had failed me, and I'd developed a new-found love for homeopathic medicine, so while I was prepared for a lengthy time commitment, I was hopeful that she would eventually be able to help me.

Early on, Amy also encouraged me to see a psychiatrist, someone who could provide anxiety medications. I asked her never to bring that topic up again. While I could sense her distaste for my opposition, she agreed.

Sure, my response was a little close minded, especially since I was paying for her opinion. But I didn't want to be dependent on medications, which could have ugly side effects; I wanted to be dependent on *me*. I didn't want those chemicals in my body. And I absolutely did not want to be someone who needed a shrink. I was already seeing a psychologist, someone to talk to, but a *psychiatrist*? Lying on that couch would mean that I was abnormal or even crazy. It reminded me of the special education classes I was thrown into when my teachers didn't know what to do with me, and if the alternative to such humiliation was not sleeping, I was prepared to choose insomnia. I just wanted to be "normal."

A year into therapy with Amy, my nocturnal anxiety worsened. I carefully crafted the perfect evening routine: a half-hour or so of reading, followed by journaling and finally a little meditation. By the time I got into bed, I was relaxed. In less than five minutes, my body would begin to fall asleep. Then, just as I crossed the brink into sublime unconsciousness, a surge of anxiety would come out of nowhere and adrenaline would run through my entire body as though I had just narrowly escaped a car accident. I'd climb out of bed and begin my relaxation routine again, but it almost never worked on the encore.

I was frustrated and desperate to find a solution. It was even affecting my professional speaking career. When I was rested, speaking was fairly easy. When I wasn't, I was more easily agitated and less effective in getting my message across. And if I couldn't do that, there was no way I could inspire the transformation I longed to create for my audiences. Something had to give.

Amy had an idea. "Misti, I know you asked me not to bring this up again," she said. "But it seems like the many things you're doing aren't working. Maybe medication will help."

I insisted I would do this on my own. "I'll figure out what I need to help myself in good time," I told her. In good time? Ha. I'd been trying for a decade and getting nowhere.

She suggested that I check out a book called *Brain Lock*, which would help me understand how the brain works and how medication could help correct the chemical imbalances causing my anxiety. I wrote down the title to appease her, but I left there resolved to find another solution.

As I sat on my meditation mat that evening, I prayed, "Please God, help me with my sleeping problems … please."

In a sudden moment of clarity, I felt like God smacked me on the back of the head and said, "I've been trying to help you, but you're not listening to anyone." How in the world did She know I am so hard-headed?

"Medication?" I asked "Are you serious?" Yes, I was having a full-blown conversation with God out loud on my meditation mat in my bedroom. What can I say? Some people need dialogue to get the message. And I am a champion conversationalist.

Suddenly, I remembered the fable about a guy whose house was about to flood. Everyone in the area had already vacated their homes. But this guy believed God would save him from the storm. He stayed in his house and prayed, "Please God, keep me safe from the flood."

Just before the waters came, a Jeep pulled up and the driver said, "Get in, sir. The water will be here in no time."

"No, I'm staying," he said. "God will save me."

As the water began to fill his home, a rescue boat passed by. "Jump in, sir," urged his saviors.

"No, I'm staying," he said. "God will save me."

Before long the water was so high that the gentleman was forced to do his praying on the roof. Within minutes, a helicopter appeared overhead and dropped down a rope ladder. "Climb up, sir," these rescuers called.

But again he said, "No, I'm staying. God will save me."

A few minutes later, the flood washed him away. The man met God at the pearly gates and exclaimed, "I prayed and prayed, God. Why didn't you save me?"

And God said, "I sent you a Jeep, a boat *and* a helicopter."

The answer had been right in front of me all along and was suggested again and again by experts I trusted – medication. The next day I ordered *Brain Lock*, by Jeffery M. Schwartz, which gave me a fairly clear understanding of how the synapses work within the brain. I learned that my brain was "miss-firing" in the evening, just before I went to sleep, kicking off my anxiety. More importantly, I learned that what was happening to me had a scientific, biochemical explanation, which is the reason many people see psychiatrists and take the stigmatized medications. As a culture, we have no problem seeing a doctor when chemical imbalances in our stomachs create indigestion. But when chemical imbalances in our brains create anxiety, clinical depression or a host of other conditions, many people still believe the trouble is a result of emotional or mental weakness, and seeking help is still taboo.

With a greater understanding of what was happening to me, I scheduled an appointment with a professional Amy recommended and persuaded Francesca to accompany me. As we quietly took our seats in the waiting area, I truly hoped no one would notice or talk to me. While there might be something wrong with *them*, I was fine. "Just here for a little education," I said to myself as I flipped the switch under my doctor's name to let him know I was in the waiting room.

Within minutes, a younger gentleman in mismatched clothes with his shirt halfway untucked, hair sticking up on one side and a goofy smile, appeared and called out my name. I shot Francesca a look that said, "You're coming with me, right!"

She smiled and said, "You got it, Misti. Go ahead. I'll wait." Because we hadn't discussed how involved she would be in this process, I couldn't argue with her, not with him standing there. I slowly got up, my heart racing, and headed down a short hallway to his office. He signaled for me to sit on one of the loveseats in his office, while he settled on a matching one across from me. He casually threw his feet up on the ottoman, pushed himself back into the couch and looked over at me. Had I not been so nervous, I would have laughed. So, *that* was why his hair stood up on one side.

He opened a file of sorts and began asking me a myriad of questions about my history. I did my best to answer, but I was too distracted by my seat to focus. The couch was so old that the cushions slipped every time I moved, leaving me sitting on a piece of wood. The physical and emotional discomfort was too much. Suddenly, I found this question pinging around inside my head: "What's funny about this?" And I knew just how to make this embarrassing situation a little more comfortable. I kicked off my shoes, pushed the cushion back under me, sat on my feet and said, "Dude, seriously, you need new couches."

"You offering to pay?" he responded quickly, a hint of a smile on his lips.

"Nope, but I advocate very strongly for new ones." We laughed, and that made me feel comfortable enough to be a little more real. "Do you have any idea how uncomfortable I already am? I mean, I couldn't even come here by myself. That's my partner in the waiting room. She's here, because I'm scared."

"Would you like to invite her back here?" he asked without another reference to the stupid old couches. I told him I was fine and we should just get through it.

He diagnosed me with post-traumatic stress disorder and obsessive-compulsive tendencies and encouraged me to take two medications – one to help with anxiety in the evenings and one for the OCD. "I'm not comfortable taking medication on a regular basis, Dr. Lorenzi," I told him. "Don't you have something I can take *only* when I absolutely need it?"

"Yes, and I will send you home with that prescription too," he said. "But with your obsessive tendencies, you're likely to end up worrying about how often you're taking the medicine and making the anxiety worse."

I was appalled by his presumptuousness. He didn't even know me. He talked to me for all of 20 minutes and was already prepared to call me obsessive. The audacity! But I kept my mouth shut, because in truth, I knew that he was onto something. I *did* insist on keeping the toothpaste label facing outward on the bathroom sink. My underwear needed to be neatly folded in the drawer, and my nightly routine was so important to me I rarely went out in the evenings. "That's fine," I said. "I'll take your three prescriptions, fill just the one and we'll see how it goes."

Two days later, I called Dr. Lorenzi to admit that he was right. I filled the other two prescriptions. Turns out, the first medication was my boat and the second two were my helicopter. It took no time for the evening medication to kick in and only weeks for the daytime medication to start helping. Finally, I could rest.

Of course, the medication meant no alcohol – a warning most people ignore. I come from a long line of alcoholics and lately I'd become concerned by the fact that I wanted a glass of wine (or three) every evening. Francesca and I had just moved in together, and the transition to being under the same roof was stressful for both of us. Sweet red wine was making it easier, and that in itself was disconcerting. So, when I heard that alcohol would make the medication ineffective and possibly worsen my anxiety, I was sold. No more booze for this Burmeister.

I still have my evening ritual of meditation, reading and writing time, and I've continued with therapy, all of which have helped me keep my dosage steady for years. I pray that, within the next few years, my brain will have re-wired itself enough that I can release the medication. If not, I have no judgment of that either.

I am learning to trust the Universe to give me the signs I need to make such decisions in my life. I listen more intently and watch more closely to see how my prayers are answered, knowing that it may not happen in the way I expect. Sometimes an answered prayer is a lesson about the truth of a situation, or more likely, a truth about ourselves.

> ### try this:
>
> *Sometimes prayers are answered in ways we least expect (like a threatening sister), or in ways we may even resist at first (like medication). Reflect and journal on a prayer you've had answered in a way you never expected, or a solution you've stumbled upon by accident.*

COMPASSION FOR THE LIAR:
FACING THE TRUTH WITHIN

The question glared at me from the screen, and under its scrutiny, I suddenly felt sick. I was reviewing comments on an early draft of this book from one of my editors, who had posed a seemingly innocuous question: "Do you want to expand on your experiences with gangs?"

I searched my mind for what I could make up in response to her inquiry then kicked myself for having gotten myself into this position. This book is about my truth, but in this case, the truth was that I had lied. For years, I lied about being in a gang, because it sounded more interesting and "cool" than saying I'd been raped, had sex with many random strangers, stolen my fair share of "stuff," considered killing myself on many occasions and spent plenty of time telling the judge, "I didn't do it," when, in fact, I had. My lie became so deep-seated that I'd almost forgotten it *was* a lie, so I put a passing reference to it in the first draft out of habit. But because it wasn't true, there was nothing to expand on, and that blasted question was now calling me out, forcing me to acknowledge that I'd let fiction creep into my non-fiction.

But just leaving it out wasn't an option. For one thing, such an omission would undermine the integrity of my journey and my book, even if no one ever knew the truth but me. Also, those closest to me believed this was part of my story and would probably notice if I never even mentioned it. The problem with lies is that they grow beyond your control, and suddenly so many people know the story that admitting the truth means losing face with (and maybe even the trust of) everyone you care about.

Having already told Francesca about my "gang experiences," I was terrified to expose the truth. I tortured myself with a million what-ifs: What if she freaks out on me? What if she leaves me because I lied to her? What if she questions everything I say from now on?

At first, she was hurt and perturbed. "That's like me telling you I never grew up in Italy," she said when I'd finished telling her what a big, fat liar I was.

I wanted to protect myself, but I knew there was no point. I'd told her the truth, and the ball was in her court. I was prepared(ish) to accept the consequences. She would either embrace the revealing and shedding of this layer or she would reject it. Later that day, she expressed her love and forgiveness in the best way she knew how, considering that I was still in the doghouse. She said, "You're brave for addressing this."

At first, those words made me feel better, but only for a little while. For some reason, the pain of shedding this layer felt worse than shedding the layer of my early sexual experiences.

Initially, I wanted to reject the reality of my truth, refusing to believe that I could ever do such a thing. Lying? Even into my adult years, when I should have known better? "Should" or "shouldn't" seem irrelevant now. I have chosen to allow the layers to emerge, and I am embracing them as part of my journey. I can never go back and re-create the beginning of my life. "Life can only be understood backwards," says the philosopher Kierkegaard, "but must be lived forwards." Thank goodness! Reflecting on where I've been and how I've grown, I can shift and re-create from here, trusting that the right people will stick around, even if others slip away.

Naturally, this level of trust did not come over night, nor is it with me all of the time. It's a gift I give to myself – permission to live in the present moment.

In his book, *The Four Agreements,* don Miguel Ruiz writes:

> *We are born perfect, and we will die perfect. The problem is that we create that character in our story that we pretend to be, or that we want to be, and we cannot hide that from ourselves. We know that we are pretending to be what we are not in the name of perfection.*

This pretense results in what Ruiz calls "lies," and he points out that while the lies are often necessary for emotional survival, all the pretending can get in the way of living an authentic life in which we are true to ourselves and honest with others. When I came up against one of my own lies, I had to decide if I was ready to be truthful. It wasn't fun, but it was a necessary part of my journey.

I'm certain there are more layers I'll need to shed. I'm not yet conscious of them, but I know they will eventually fall away, and I'm hoping that when they do, I will spend less time judging myself and more time reflecting on how that awareness can help me grow in the present.

Samantha, my therapist at that time, helped me see the value of this particular layer. "We don't know why, Misti, but for some reason those lies helped you to survive," she explained. "Be grateful for them and allow them to fall to the side. You simply don't need them any longer."

My journey has revealed over and over that when we work to shed our fears, and all of the protective titles and fiction, we are able to love the person we see in the mirror, or the image of ourselves that others reflect back to us, warts and all.

WARTS AND ALL: AN UNLIKELY MIRROR

I met Rich at a community meeting on leadership in 2006. We hit it off so well that we set a time for coffee the following week. Soon, we were almost inseparable.

Over the next two years, Rich and I questioned life together and challenged and supported each other in personal and professional endeavors. I even asked him to help me launch a local group focused on innovative leadership with another great friend and colleague, Sophia.

We had fun together. I remember a particularly special day we shared on his speed boat. Because we both had flexible schedules, we planned our trip during the week, so we pretty much had the lake to ourselves. The water was calm and the sun was warm on our backs. When we got too hot, we'd jump into the water for a few minutes, swim around and try dunking each other. As evening approached, we laid on the back, cushiony part of the boat staring up at the sky and discussed our hopes and dreams. He shared the characteristics he sought in a woman. He was so full with love that I could feel his real desire to have someone to share it with – and I wanted that for him more than anything.

A few weeks before my birthday in 2008, Rich met a beautiful woman at an art gallery who happened to be friends with Sophia. His house – complete with pool, sunroom and other entertaining perks – was the perfect place for my May birthday party, which he volunteered to host. Eager to see Rich happy, I asked Sophia to invite her friend. Sparks flew. The budding couple talked to each other most of the evening and ended it in the hot tub with his arm around her. They were soon dating.

Naturally, he began spending the majority of his time with the new love of his life, and less and less with me – which made perfect sense. But after a few months, I started feeling disconnected from my best friend. My gut told me something was wrong, that it wasn't just his "honeymoon" period keeping him away from me. He was short with me when we spoke on the phone and he barely acknowledged my e-mails. This wasn't normal. So, on one particularly tense call, I asked him if everything was OK.

"I'm good," he answered quickly, a little too quickly. I probed further, but all he would say was that we should speak in person.

A sharp feeling of abandonment, a trusty companion from my child-hood, surfaced in a fierce way. "He's angry with me for something I did or didn't do and now he's going to go away," were the words that echoed in my head until I saw him. He came over the day before Francesca and I were set to host a party at his house for him and his new girlfriend, whose birthdays happen to be a few days apart. I was eager to hear what was on his mind. My heart racing from the suspense, I started, "What's up, Rich?"

For the next two hours he downloaded two years worth of pent-up irri-tations with me, chronicling my every "sin" against him, issues he'd never mentioned before. "Remember that time I was supposed to pick you up from the airport when you came home from Greece? I couldn't make it so I paid to have a shuttle bus take you home. When I asked you about your ride, you only said, 'It took four hours. We were the last to be dropped off.'"

And the beating continued with enough one-two punches to take out a heavy-weight champion. He presented every bit of evidence he could scrape up to make his case: I was a selfish, manipulative, self-centered per-son. Barely able to stop myself from bursting into tears, I went into me-diation mode, using all the tricks I'd learned for effective communication to steer the conversation into a healthier place. "Rich," I started. "What I'm hearing you say is…" I repeated his words. "Did I get it?"

"Yes."

"Is there more?"

My heart sank as he geared up for round two, which included more examples to prove he was *right*. I asked him to move away from "you" statements and focus on "I" statements. I even gave him an example: "Misti, when you do this, I feel this," rather than, "You are this."

"Misti, if I polled 100 people, they would all say these things are true about you," he assured me.

I wanted to scream, "Are you out of your mind? Not everyone sees the world or my actions the same way you do. Your view is coming solely from your own experience of life." But I stayed calm. After two hours of trying to understand where he was coming from (and trying not to slap some sense into him) I eventually agreed to look at all of the things he said were true about me and consider how I could change. It was excruciating to give in like that, but I knew there was little I could say in this situation, when all my defenses were up, to create an empowering conversation.

Knowing I could not continue feeling so close to someone who talked to me that way, I managed a cordial goodbye, knowing I had lost one of my best friends. Despite Francesca's impassioned protests, I insisted on hosting the party the next day. Bailing on the people I'd invited didn't feel right. Everyone would have known something was wrong and might have even asked him about it. I didn't want to give him any reason to share his awful opinion of me with anyone else.

When we spoke on the phone a few days later, I had made peace(ish) with my hurt and was finally in a place to listen, but only with some very important boundaries in place. "Rich, you can always share ideas for my growth," I explained. "I welcome such feedback. You can let me know that when I do certain things, you feel a certain way. I want to be a great friend and I'm happy to adjust to come across better in your world. Our friendship is very important to me, and I'm committed to working this out. But you are never allowed to tell me I *am* any of the words you called me."

"I held back telling my truth for two years, Misti," he said defensively.

"You should be *happy* that I finally shared. I am going to share in the way I know how – take it or leave it. If I polled 100 people, they'd all say I'm right." We obviously weren't making progress if he was dragging that one out again. I had to deliver a speech that day, so we needed to get off the phone before I got upset again – or devised a plan to take out his knee caps without getting caught.

"Clearly, we are not going to find a resolution on this call," I said. "Let's give this some space and reconnect another day." After that call we only communicated when necessary, usually regarding some business item.

It wasn't until a year later that I took the time to seriously ponder Rich's diatribe – this time from a place of peace. While in Bali, Indonesia, for my honeymoon, I got up early one morning, grabbed my journal and my copy of *Loving What Is* by Byron Katie and headed to my new favorite restaurant to read. Like most restaurants in Bali, this one was outdoors – right next to the ocean.

Breakfast was delicious. The eggs in Bali are a deep orange with a strong yoke flavor that comes from completely free-range chickens. And the toast at this restaurant was made fresh every morning. As I enjoyed my feast, I noticed the bluish-green of the ocean, the bright azure sky and a beautiful mountain off in the distance, I thought about what I had just read. Katie writes about accepting what others have to say about us, uncovering the truth of it and embracing it without judgments about "right" or "wrong."

Rich came to mind. I grabbed my journal and began writing all the thoughts running through my mind. And for the first time I wasn't over-

> **try this:**
> *Make a list of at least five traits you see in yourself that you (or others) might consider "bad." Try to suspend judgment of them and write about how those traits have been useful to you in the past. Ask yourself, what is it that these traits protect? In your everyday life, how can you create a safe space for that treasure?*

whelmed with an immediate sense of anger. "Selfish. Is that true about me?" I pondered. My answer was quick and it felt right. Yes, sometimes. "Manipulative? Have I been *this* way before? Is it a part of me?" Yep.

I examined each of the many things Rich said about me, and each time I decided, "Yes, I *can* be that way." What was it, then, that made me so angry when Rich shared with me that day?

I took a deep breath and looked up. I watched women walking by with huge baskets on their heads and someone sweeping (in Bali, someone is always sweeping), and once again, the ocean and sky met right at the edge of the volcano. I felt so safe in this place, and a sense of peace came over me. Everything seemed objective, as though nothing could be wrong in that moment.

Rich's words had generated such anger and hurt because I thought those things he was saying about me were *bad*, really bad. I did not want to identify with any of those traits, yet all of them are part of me.

"But are they really *bad*?" I asked myself. The answer brought with it a wave of peace. No. Neither are all of my perceivably positive traits always positive. It's not about "good" or "bad." It's simply part of my layers – and my protective mechanisms. When I'm behaving selfishly, it's proba- bly because I'm not taking care of my needs, or perhaps because I don't know how to be generous in the way this person prefers to receive gen- erosity. When I feel out of control (which, with two alcoholic parents, is how I felt most of my life), my natural tendency is to want to control and manipulate . It's all a subconscious intention to create a safe space.

In reality, everything is already safe, and there's no need to be manipu- lative, even under the harshest of conditions. While those things may be true of me at times, I don't think they are true to my authentic self, so I *want* to release my need to rely on them, which takes awareness. When it's brought to my attention, either from self-reflection and being present to myself or from someone I trust, I can alter my behavior to reflect the person I truly am – underneath any fear or insecurities.

It all made sense and, suddenly, I felt a huge weight lifted from my shoulders. Instead of being angry at Rich, I was grateful that he led me to a part of myself I did not fully love just yet. Each time I found acceptance for another part of me, I also found gratitude and joy.

Upon my return from Bali, I asked Rich to coffee. Before I left that morning, I took the time to clear my mind of all expectations from him. I knew what *I* wanted to say, and I was open to any further enlightenment that might come from this conversation.

Soon after we sat down, tea in hand, I said, "Rich, I want you to know how much I appreciate you for sharing everything you shared, in exactly the way you shared it." He shifted in his chair and looked around nervously, probably planning his exit strategy in case I'd lost my mind and was about to attack him. He'd been preparing for battle and didn't know how to respond to this unexpected maneuver.

To ease the discomfort and clarify my intentions, I said, "I have no expectations of you. I simply want you to know how grateful I am. All those things you said about me are true. I had no idea there were parts of me that I didn't accept, so by bringing them to my attention, you've helped me learn to love *all* of me."

Not yet ready to share a peace pipe, he shifted again and unloaded some of the weapons he'd armed himself with for our meeting – a list of a few more things I had done before leaving for Bali that he did not like. Good, he had made some progress of his own lately. Expressing his dislike for such *recent* offenses was kind of a breakthrough for him. I acknowledged him and made sure he knew that I will always love him. "I have love for you too," he said. I'm not sure what that means, but it doesn't matter. My mission impossible –

try this:
Write for 10 minutes as if you had only 10 minutes to live. What happens when we let go of fear, shed all our protective entrapments and live in the present with who we really are?

to authentically share my love with someone who hurt me – was accomplished.

With that, we went on with life as usual, only communicating when necessary. Now, when I see him, he is like a mirror for my emotions. I can always tell where I am with my personal growth by how I react to his presence, though *he* typically acts the same way – aloof and disconnected. When I am feeling centered and present, nothing he does or says bothers me. In fact, I wish him well. Other times, I find myself avoiding him at all costs, or wanting to throw eggs at his house.

When I'm feeling anything other than at peace around him, I know I'm in a place of fear. In these instances, I bring myself back to the present by calling a friend to chat, listing all of the things I am grateful for that day, meditating, reading an inspirational quote or texting loved ones just to let them know how much I appreciate them.

But ultimately, everything I said to him was true. I *am* grateful for the unlikely gift he gave me. It wasn't what he said; it was the *way* he said it. Sure, if he had been a bit more diplomatic and compassionate, I would have listened and made changes because I cared for him, which would also have brought me closer to myself. I wish he had done so, because I would still have my friend. But the pain and reflection that his tactless delivery inspired forced me to dig deeper, to reflect and uncover *why* these things were part of me, and to embrace them.

Elisabeth Kübler-Ross wrote that there are only two emotions – love and fear. All positive emotions come from love, and all negative ones come from fear. And the two cannot co-exist. As she put it, "They're opposites. If we're in fear, we are not in a place of love. When we're in a place of love, we cannot be in a place of fear."

We cannot do anything about what happened in the past or what will happen in the future, so focusing on either makes many of us fearful. But when we're truly living in the present – with all past and future fears laid aside – we're left with love.

interlude
"STARBURSTS"

Sound asleep …
Loud, thunderous explosions all around me –
To be expected at preciously 12:01am, January 1st.
Frightening and irritating nonetheless
Joyful emotions scattered at the end of each starburst.
Covering my ears, hoping it would soon end.

A closure to the year – the ringing in of new beginnings
Praying that was the final explosion
Wanting deep inside to experience the release of the past –
The promise of great experiences to come
The sky fully lit for moments at a time
Little footsteps rushing to witness the beauty
Is it over yet?

An even bigger, louder, thunder of vibrant light
Almost as if neighbors were competing
Competing with my desires, no doubt
Fully triggered by nonsensical fear
Bravely fought off all such desires
Fear fully engage ~ rational thought vanished
Replaced with empty desire

Releasing judgment
Locating humor beneath these layers
Trusting in this experience
Feeling the fireworks bursting inside
Freedom right here
in this moment.

stage two
Guides Along the Way

TRANSFORMATION:
From Insecurity to Self-Esteem

"We do not believe in ourselves until someone reveals that deep inside us is valuable, worth listening to, worthy of our trust, sacred to our touch. Once we believe in ourselves we can risk curiosity, wonder, spontaneous delight or any experience that reveals the human spirit."

E.E. CUMMINGS

In her book, *Sacred Contracts,* Carolyn Myss writes, "To love yourself, truly love yourself, is to finally discover the essence of personal courage, self-respect, integrity, and self-esteem. These are the qualities of grace that come directly from a soul with stamina." As I journey inward to heal the child and unearth the hero underneath all the layers of insecurity, fear, judgment, and even my own masks and misconceptions about who I am, I find myself traveling to a place of self-love. I don't mean the type of narcissistic love that feeds the ego; I mean the type of compassionate and accepting love that feeds the soul.

I would not have found my way to this place without guides and mentors along the way, heroes who have seen me for who I am, even when I acted unkindly to them and put up walls to protect myself.

Joseph Campbell speaks of a turning point in the hero's journey, one where she "discovers for the first time that there is a benign power everywhere supporting [her] in [her] superhuman passage." To be willing to make this journey of self-knowledge and acceptance has required a soul with stamina, but my soul has had plenty of help – from the girls who beat me up in middle school, to the teachers who saw me as more than a troublemaker, the strangers who showed me generosity without strings, and a few treasured friends who brought love, wisdom and even poetry to my quest. The following stories highlight just a few of the heroes who have made my quest – and my life – one of beauty and purpose.

FIGHT OR FLIGHT

As each class period neared its end, my stomach muscles would begin to tighten and fear would take over. I knew the minute I walked out of the classroom I'd be accosted by a group of girls with nothing better to do than to torment me. While I did everything in my power to avoid them, these girls would meet me in the same general location on my way home almost every day and constantly pick fights. Is seventh grade that much fun for everyone?

My brother, Lance, had specific instructions from my father to watch out for me and stop any tormenting, but one day he decided to make me deal with them alone. As we rounded the corner and made our way past the gas station, about three-fourths of the way home, I looked into the distance and noticed three girls making their way toward me. One of them had already made it clear during school that she intended to kick my … well, you know.

I picked up the pace. We passed the gas station; a couple more blocks and we'd be home safe. That's when they caught up to us. I headed for a nearby alley that would shorten the distance between the current danger and safety, but Lance continued walking straight. I considered making a run for it, but I knew that would only make me look like a wimp. I didn't want to be made fun of in school for that, too, so I just walked quickly.

Within my first 10 steps into the alley – a space that ran between the chain-link fences that enclosed the back yards of our neighbors' homes – the girls surrounded me. And the fists began flying. Lance made his way over to us before anyone got seriously hurt, and as he began to pull the girls off of me, I thought I was rescued. Nope. He took care of two of the girls, apparently feeling that the fight was "fair" as long it was one on one.

My opponent and I both walked away with a few bruises but no permanent damage. I remember feeling like I'd won, but in truth, I was mostly just proud that she didn't clobber me.

I was hurt and angry with Lance, but when I asked him why he didn't defend me, he said, "I knew you could handle them." And suddenly, I knew it too. I never liked fighting, but the experience made me feel much more confident, which was useful in the many fights that later ensued.

Most times back then, I just wanted to hide from my tormentors. When I hit a teacher whom I'd warned not to touch me, I earned myself a one-way ticket to a place that allowed me to do just that – my grammar school's special education program. Sure, I already knew that one plus one equals two, could physically feed myself and was the only student in this class without mental or physical handicaps, but at least I was mostly out of harm's way during school hours. And when I behaved well, my teachers took me to McDonald's. Before long, they began suggesting I go back into regular classes. Like them, I knew deep down that this program was wrong for me, but I was managing to get some one-on-one attention and there was no student in there capable of fighting with me.

When my parents later relocated us to Crook, Colorado, where there weren't as many fights (maybe because there weren't as many kids), I was put into regular classes again, except for a few hours in the middle of the day when I'd be separated from my 14 classmates and placed in a small room with one woman, Linda, for a special education class. Being singled out and again given the stigma of "special ed" was terrible for my self-esteem, and I reacted with anger. I hated Linda, this woman I considered a symbol of my stupidity and inadequacy, and I wasn't afraid to show it.

The first six months must have been horrifying for Linda, as I would simply get up in the middle of our lesson and walk out of her office. When she'd try to stop me, I would physically push her away. But she never stopped trying to engage me, to converse with me, to befriend me. During home football games, she even encouraged me to sit with her family.

I rejected her many times; yet, miraculously, I never heard about any of this from my mother. Linda chose to deal with me on her own, rather than pushing me off to the administration.

One day, while trying to push Linda out of my way, I accidently hit her in the arm. Having made that mistake once before, I was terrified about what would happen next, so I ran from her. She came running after and caught me. She wrapped her arms around me and just held on – tightly. I could not see her face, but I can imagine her expression based on the reactions of other teachers, who came out to help, surveyed the situation and then slowly walked away. I struggled to escape her embrace, but her grip was too tight. Eventually, I gave in. When she finally let me pull away enough to see her face, there was only kindness in her eyes. "Ready to finish our lesson?" she asked at last. I agreed, and off we went.

Linda was an Asian woman who lived in a small, all-white town with her white husband and two children. I can imagine she knew how it felt to be discriminated against, even ostracized, and she was committed to helping me feel loved unconditionally. She was the first person who showed me such fierce kindness, and over time, her persistence penetrated my exterior shell. She had no underlying agenda; she simply wanted to help, and eventually, I was ready to receive her love.

Joseph Campbell writes that on the journey, at a crucial moment when the hero needs aid, she usually meets a guide or mentor to help her get to the next destination on her path. Linda filled this role for me. Over time, her unconditional acceptance worked wonders on my confidence.

CARBURETOR CONFIDENCE

Whenever I wanted to get away from everything, I would take my motorbike (a 60-cc engine) and drive up the dirt roads near our home, careful not to go too far. I'd make my way to the middle of a corn field, where I would sit and enjoy the calm air and the tall rows that hid me from the world. Mostly, I liked riding around. I was 15 years old, and that motor-cycle was my only way to get away from it all, a freedom most budding adults yearn for but few actually experience without a driver's license.

To start the engine, I had to kick down hard and fast on a small lever several times. After a few kicks, it would usually fire up, and I would be off for at least a couple of hours. But one day, I couldn't start the bike. Thankfully, my father was a mechanic, so I set off in search of him, sure he would be willing and able to fix it for me.

He took a quick look and said the carburetor needed to be cleaned. "OK," I said to him, thinking to myself, *Well, what are you waiting for?* I never liked getting my hands covered in grease, nor did I know what to do with a carburetor. And this *was* his skill set. But something in Dad's face told me that he wasn't going to do it for me this time.

He said he'd help get the carburetor off the bike, but I would have to clean it out. I wasn't happy about this arrangement, but I knew I'd be even less happy sitting around the house all day, so I agreed. We took it into the kitchen, along with the proper tools.

Carburetors are complex, and I was terrified to take it apart, afraid I would mess it up or be unable to get it back together. But at least I'd have my father standing there to tell me if I was on the wrong track. Wrong again. As my father walked away, I stammered, "Dad, you do know how to put this back together, right?"

He chuckled as the screen door slammed behind him. I wanted my mo-torbike to work but if I didn't do this right, I would surely never ride again. I stared at it for a few minutes, hoping he'd come back and tell me the joke was over. "Good one, Dad," I'd say. "I'll be in my room when you're finished. You're the best!"

But when he didn't come back, I had to face facts – I was really on my own. I could give it a shot and risk messing it up, or just go ahead and park it for good. I began to take it apart, carefully placing the *many* pieces onto the counter to help me remember where they went. This seemed like a good strategy, but after dismantling and cleaning everything, I had no clue where they all went. Confused and overwhelmed, I sat staring at the pile of small parts, certain I'd never ride again.

That's when Dad came back. He knew exactly how to put it back together and showed me the way. What had seemed absolutely impossible was now something I had conquered. What had felt like abandonment in a moment when I needed support was actually a self-confidence boost I desperately needed. Instead of being my hero, rushing in to save the day, Dad taught me how to be my own hero. Instead of just giving me the freedom I so treasured, he made me work for it; in essence, he helped me free myself.

Sometimes simply knowing that someone else sees potential in you, believes that you can do something even *you* believe is beyond you, is better than all the help in the world. He taught me that with a little jump start, and some guidance and support when I got stuck, I could do whatever I set my mind to. And the wind on my face never felt as sweet as it did that day.

A few years ago, while visiting Colorado, I went back to that old dirt road. I took a photo,

try this:

Think back to a place where, in your youth, you went to "get away." Try to remember how it felt to experience that freedom. Describe it — and the feeling you had when you went there.

which I had mounted and now display in my office. When I'm struggling, it helps me to remember where I came from, to appreciate how far I've come and to know that I have always been able to find peace in solitude, in nature and in freedom, no matter how challenging my life may get at times.

TRANSFORMATION:
From Being Seen to Seeing

"Face your life story with love, and you will
experience the most incredible dream quest."

DON MIGUEL RUIZ

Every good journey, in fiction and real life, involves faithful companions. Harry Potter had his best buddies; Socrates had his students;
Dorothy had her crew. I, too, have enjoyed the company of many faithful friends along the way. But before I was able to welcome their friendship, I needed to settle things within myself and reconcile with a neglected
companion who had been there all along – my inner child. Now that I am
learning how to get over being annoyed with her for always tugging at
my sleeve and whining, and I am actually attending to her needs, she is
proving invaluable. As my adult self learns how to make peace, even build
a relationship with that little irrepressible child, I am able to look at us in
the mirror and face our multi-faceted being with love as we embark on
this incredible quest.

ARE THE FISH JUMPING?

I love fishing, just not in the traditional sense. Real fish are slimy and
stinky, and I feel bad when I catch one, even if I'm ultimately going to un-
hook and set it free. However, while I haven't always wanted to admit it, I
do enjoy fishing for compliments. I'm quite adept at it, actually. After many
years of practice, I should be. But it took me a long time to learn that my
brand of fishing has one (and maybe only the one) thing in common with
the old-fashioned kind – if you're not discriminating about where you cast
your line, you usually wind up disappointed and frustrated.

Sometimes I go fishing in ponds filled with beautiful fish, and the pay-off is amazing. But more often, I find myself empty-handed because I have been stubborn and expected certain people to fill this role for me, even when I'd found their ponds empty again and again in the past. All of my life, I remember asking my parents, "Am I beautiful?" "Do you think I'm smart?" "Is my body nice-looking?" "Am I good at sports?" or any other bait I could think of to toss at them. While they occasionally would bite and give a compliment or two where it made the most sense to them, my mother would usually say, "You're fishing in the wrong pond."

Don't worry; this is not the part where I lie back on my therapist's couch, prop up my feet and spend the next hour blaming my mother for all my life's problems (not to say I *haven't* done that!). Still, mothers are who most young girls look to for their earliest affirming mirrors. In the reflection of their mothers' praise, feedback and kindness, they see who they are and will be. As a child, I walked away feeling rejected and angry when I heard those dreadful, uncaring words. And until recently, my adult self despised them just as much.

Early in 2010, I spoke at my grandmother's funeral. After the service, many people approached me and offered exceedingly kind and complimentary words about my speech. My mother, however, said nothing to me about it.

During the lunch following the service, I sat between my mother and her sister. My mother leaned across me and said to my aunt, "That's the first time I've ever heard Misti speak in public." My heart began to race. I couldn't wait to hear what she was going to say about it. Sure, it was a small funeral, not the crowds I'm used to addressing, but it was close enough, and the content was certainly meaningful to us both. I waited for her to add something like, "And WOW, it was fantastic!"

Nope. There was silence, followed by a new topic. I was disappointed. Aware of my need to hear something more from my mom, I took about an hour and gathered my thoughts – in the ladies room! I sat on the toilet contemplating whether I should ask my mom for more. "What do I expect to hear from her?" I asked myself. For some strange reason, that particular toilet offered little peace that day.

As we were saying goodbye, I couldn't help but ask what it was like for her to see me speak for the first time. "Fine," she said sharply, followed by a short silence. "That's all you're gonna get from me."

My heart sank. I felt my face flush with embarrassment, afraid that others had heard me asking for words of affirmation and were now judging my need. At the same time, my mind was racing to think of something to say that would perhaps evoke a different, more satisfying response. But there was nothing more to say. "Perfect," I lied and turned away from her.

Later, as I drove to the airport, those words – "You're fishing in the wrong pond" – kept echoing through my mind. There was a sea filled with acknowledgement; yet, I insisted on fishing in a pond I knew to be empty. But she's my mom and she *should* at least say "Thank you," shouldn't she? My reality? She didn't. Why?

I suppose the answer to that question is less important than my greater realization: Feedback from others is a brilliant way to gain clarity around our gifts and skills. We need good mirrors in which we can see ourselves in an accurate (and positive) light, and to know that other people think and care about our existence enough to offer kind and supportive words. And sure, sometimes we just need our egos stroked a bit. But I should be like the experienced fisher who doesn't waste her time on ponds she knows to be empty. In other words, I should give whatever affirmation I have to give, and only ask for it from those eager to share compliments. Now, before seeking validation from others, my first question to myself is: "How beautiful are the fish in this pond?"

While I used to despise the words "You're fishing in the wrong pond," I've come to appreciate them. Is it "right" or "wrong" that my parents were unable to give me what I needed in that time and space? That question is akin to asking if it is wrong that some ponds have no fish and others are so full that the fish are jumping? The simple answer is no. The better question is, who is so full with self-love that they have extra to offer? Go fishing there!

And remember to throw a few back to keep those ponds full. While fishing for compliments might seem a little self-absorbed, the give and take, the *mirroring* of encouragement and compassion, is crucial in relationships. Like in the biblical story of the loaves and fish, good words multiply the more they are shared.

try this:

Make a list of the possible "ponds" in your life — those that are full and those that are empty. Beside each pond, or inside, write the compliments and praise you can throw in for that person.

There are many ponds into which I enjoy throwing a fish or two on a regular basis. Sometimes I catch a few fish from these same ponds; other times I don't. I've learned that giving with no strings attached leaves me feeling free to worry about things that are important.

THE TRANSFORMATION OF COMPASSION: A SHIFT IN PERSPECTIVE

During my undergraduate years at the University of Northern Colorado, one of my mentors, Cynthia, listened as I shared about my struggles with my mom. I will always remember her insight: "Misti, think for a moment of your mother as a child who has a mom."

Suddenly, I was free from the grip many of my stories had on me. If my mother was once a little girl who had a mother, then she probably had her own challenges and issues. She had her own needs and desires too. So, like me, like everyone, my mother wasn't perfect. And thanks to Cynthia, I no longer needed her to be.

This new mindset has opened me to a deeper level of love for all people, whether they leave my life or stay for a while. We were all children once and must remember that an insecure, easily-frightened, emotionally-awkward child remains inside the vast majority of us, wanting to be understood.

When I was not getting what I needed from my mother, I judged her and still felt empty. Everyone looks bad in that mirror. Why wouldn't she just say the words I so desperately needed to hear? But maybe the more important question was whether I could validate myself. I mean, sure, hearing kind words from others is always a blessing, but what if I could give those words to myself *and* feel full afterward? What if I didn't have to parade around seeking validation, like a child in desperate need of sugar?

When I see someone clearly in need of affirmation, I immediately stop, listen, affirm and do my best to inspire. Yet, when it comes to *me*, I look the other way and try to avoid my feelings. Like a seven year old, I kick myself and yell, "Hey, pay attention to me!" Instead of attending to that need, I often get my own attention by not sleeping and putting myself through mental beatings.

When I start this internal diatribe, my pond dries up, my inner child cries and I am unable to be present to see the truth of the situation or the people in front of me. I am beginning to learn the power of offering words of compassion to oneself, and becoming the mirror that can compassionately affirm the face gazing into it. I don't necessarily always do it, but, hey, at least I understand the power I hold! Rather than shoving my needs to the side, I'm learning to truly listen to myself (and my little girl) and consider how I can treat myself the same way I would treat a stranger in need of kindness.

I have had a few beautiful moments, where it felt like God was moving through me, moments where it didn't matter whether I was being seen because I was *seeing*, seeing the people in front of me, seeing the people in my life and seeing myself clearly. I know there will be more of those moments as I continue to address and comfort my little girl. It is only when I take her hand and invite her along, even when she's pitching a fit, that the hero's journey becomes possible and real.

MIRROR, MIRROR ON THE WALL

⚓

When I was younger, I wanted one of those fairytale mirrors to tell me that I, not Snow White or anyone else, was best of all. As if *anyone* is really "best of all!" No, we are *all* unique and special, just like everyone else.

On a recent drive home from couple's therapy with my partner, Francesca, where I'd fully expressed just how much affection I need to feel comfortable in a relationship, she said something that reminded me why it's important to have mirrors. "I'm imagining you as a baby," she said gently, "one who cries out for attention and is ignored." Francesca's observation made sense: I *was* the child she described.

That childish attention-monger has yet to leave me. But my need for attention doesn't always manifest in fun, harmless ways. Eight million Americans consider suicide each year. I've been one of them. During adolescence, I would often visualize myself walking up the dirt road to the railroad tracks, patiently awaiting the next train, which might stop the pain. Many years later, I began processing the pain in therapy.

I spent the vast majority of my childhood either happy or angry, never really content, comfortable or relaxed. I'm quite sure that by today's standards, I would be labeled bipolar, or as having ADD or ADHD. I couldn't have put this into words at the time, but my happiest moments were a direct result of having done something that made me look like a role model, that gave me a mirror in which I could see success reflected back at me. When I wasn't being "seen," I felt bad inside.

In her book *Kitchen Table Wisdom,* Rachel Naomi Remen cautions: "To seek approval is to have no resting place, no sanctuary. Like all judgment, approval encourages a constant striving. It makes us uncertain of who we are and our true value." Yet, as a child, I knew no other way; I had no idea such a sanctuary existed. In Remen's stories of suffering and the healing powers we all have inside of us, she shows how suspending judgment of ourselves (good or bad), is the first step to self-awareness, to understanding and the recognition of our true value.

Yes, I still say ridiculous things at inappropriate times, hoping to be seen, and thus spend entirely too much time pulling my big foot back out of my mouth. Fortunately, my reasons for needing to be seen are less important to me now, and they have little to do with the approval of others. Rather, what's most important is finding my way back to the present, appreciating opportunities that naturally surface for everyone to shine.

As I've learned to let the light shine from within, and onto others, my need for that talking, all-affirming mirror has lessened. I'm learning to release that need and just enjoy getting to know myself. And I am beginning to trust that who I am is perfect, even though I occasionally do things other people might consider annoying.

I have also come to appreciate myself for the strategies I created to help me survive during the times I've felt so isolated. Yes, I did manipulate my parents into buying me a letter jacket by insinuating that we could easily afford it if they stopped drinking for a few months. With my entire identity wrapped up in sports, I needed that jacket to define me – and I got it!

Even though I was a star athlete, my high-school grades nearly kept me out of college. I was accepted as a provisional student, but as a condition of my enrollment, I could not participate in sports for the first year. Shifting my identity from track star to geek was rough. Purposefully placing myself where I could see a smart classmate's test in college ensured I got a passing grade in that really hard class though. Well, it would have if our teacher had not given out several versions of the test (thank God she let me retake it!). With academics at the center of my new identity, I needed to do well. These are not actions I'm proud of, but I did what I thought I had to do to survive.

In his book, *The Four Agreements,* don Miguel Ruiz calls strategies we create for making reality bearable "lies," but he withholds judgment and instead, encourages self-understanding. Many of my strategies have become unnecessary as I've learned that the most important validation is inside of me. Instead of stealing a knife for my brother, I now trust that the gifts I have to offer (even if they are homemade and have worth only to me and the recipient) are perfect. Instead of looking for ways to manipulate my friends into liking me, I can be myself and trust that they will *want* to share time with me.

This, admittedly, is my greatest challenge at this time in my life. I do not want to wait for people to get to know and like me; instead, I want them to spend five minutes getting to know me at the grocery store and then invite me to their home for a meal the next day. I know it doesn't work like that; yet, I still try. These have been my defense mechanisms for a long time, and habits can be hard to break. Being aware of our habits, and having loved ones point them out in a kind way, makes it easier to avoid those familiar patterns of behavior and accept reality.

In the moment Francesca identified the crying baby within me, I was able to simply appreciate my needs. I am that crying baby, but that no longer feels like a "bad" thing. Crying babies can be soothed if you give them what they need. Only instead of reaching out to someone else for attention and affirmation, we can try new strategies to fulfill our own needs.

While I still yearn for words of affirmation, and deeper still, a beloved community in which I can thrive, understanding this need enables me to see myself and others with a little less judgment and a lot more grace, which is so much better and more honest than a talking mirror.

TRANSFORMATION:
From Isolation to Friendship

"Every one of us gets through the tough times because somebody is there, standing in the gap to close it for us."
OPRAH WINFREY

In his account of the hero's journey, Joseph Campbell says repeatedly that these quests are rarely, if ever, taken alone. As soon as the hero overcomes the blinding need to be seen and takes the first steps toward forgiveness and compassion, she sees other people and becomes able to accept aid and friendship.

Shortly after college, I found myself lying on the bathroom floor of my apartment in Bethesda, Maryland, where I had no friends and $37 in the bank. My biggest fear was not that I would never find a job; it was that I would again become that insecure little girl who went unseen, who didn't matter in the world. It was more than a fear; it was an incessant nagging. "You really are never going to amount to anything," I told myself. "You thought you had it, but now it's gone. You are a nobody now. No one cares about you. You're stupid. No one even wants to spend time with you. You're a burden to yourself and those around you."

During this time, people often said to me, "Don't give up, Misti." Don't give up on my dreams? Or don't kill myself? I wasn't sure which they meant, but to me it seemed like the same thing. To give up on finding a way to share my talents was akin to giving up on my spirit, which was like dying. I'm quite sure it would have been days, if not weeks, before anyone found me had I taken my own life (and I thought about it more than once). My family didn't know how to help me, and I had no strong friendships. What I needed was simple – community.

I didn't feel like I had a choice. It wasn't inspiration or determination that picked me up off the floor that day. It was fear – fear of fading away, once more, into worthlessness. I wanted, *needed*, to feel that I belonged. And lying on the floor, sobbing into the cracked tiles, wasn't making me feel like I belonged anywhere – except maybe an asylum.

This was before I learned to hear, value and even respect, that miserable child – the one who could defend herself, take apart a carburetor and race her motorbike all over creation. When I finally realized the necessity of giving myself a little love and care, even fleetingly and half-heartedly, I started recollecting my self-esteem. I could love myself a little more deeply and see myself a little more clearly, so I started seeing others a little more clearly as well, and recognizing that there were people out there with a message for me – namely, that I was not alone.

It took some time before I was ready for true, lasting friendships. While I *wanted* them – urgently and impatiently – I wasn't yet the friend *I* needed to be. But as I continued on the journey, I gradually found my world filled with friends more wonderful than I could have imagined. If this sounds mythic, it is. It also is the most ordinary story of the most extraordinary people.

ZIG ZIGLAR AND THE
CURE FOR LONELINESS

I had only been in the D.C. area about a year, and as I walked down those noisy streets, I was acutely aware of the irritation in the air. Motorists honked their horns at each other and at pedestrians trying to cross the street – and, frankly, at anything that was in their way. I began to notice how impatient I got while checking out at the grocery store – at the length of the lines and the slow pace of the cashiers. "Don't they see I'm in a hurry?" I fumed. "They're being slow on purpose."

I remember thinking to myself one day, "I have to get out of this town before I start acting like these people." I also remember how important it felt for me to get back to my computer as quickly as possible so that I could do something great and feel important again. I was isolated, scared and lonely. Yet, all I wanted to do was hurry back to my empty apartment.

I had not been in D.C. long enough to develop strong friendships, at least not ones intimate enough for me. I met a lot of people, but no one really *knew* me – and, I hardly knew anyone. The few times I was courageous enough to share myself (including my unabashed fears), it scared people away. The whole experience reminded me of the old notion that when life gets hard, you should share your troubles and watch to see who's left behind. There was no one left behind. Of course not! They barely knew me. I was alone and highly resentful about it. I wanted to know why, in my greatest time of need, no one was there to help me? Wasn't I a good person – someone who deserved to be loved?

Fortunately, this was during the time I was conducting informational interviews with three to five professionals a day – keeping myself busy to keep from going crazy. On our second meeting, one exceptionally generous man gave me a goal-setting CD. I'm quite certain he saw me as a lonely young woman with no direction and thought helping me focus was the answer. While he did help me learn invaluable goal-setting skills, the more important wisdom he imparted was the value of continued learning.

While I hardly had enough money to eat, I shopped for more self-help CDs. One of the first ones I bought was *A View from the Top* by Zig Ziglar. I wanted that view, so I thought I'd see if he could help me get to the mountaintop. As I drove to and from informational interviews, trying to figure out my next career move, I listened to Ziglar talk about many aspects of life. He really captured my heart, though, when he shared the secret to finding the relationships I'd yearned for: "If you want great friends, go out and be a great friend."

As painful as it was to admit, Ziglar was right; I wasn't a good friend, or I would have some. I knew I had work to do. "What does it mean to be a great friend?" I asked myself. Blank – my mind went blank.

After indulging in a short, one-woman pity-party over my shortcomings (a lonely one, I might add, because as it turns out, other people rarely RSVP for these events), I decided to put my mind to better use and begin my research. I sat in my apartment reading, writing out my goals and trying to stay focused on the moment, and an idea came to me. I would watch how people who had friends acted, imitate them and get some companions of my very own. The first thing I noticed was that people with large social circles were good listeners and attentive to other people's needs.

Before long, I began stumbling. I tried to imitate what they did and anxiously awaited the results. I did this for at least a year and made little progress. I had a couple of people I called my friends, though I wasn't sure they would stick around if I showed my fear. While I didn't realize this immediately, I was trying to be a good friend with the hopes of getting something in return.

Later, I came to realize that I truly enjoy the feeling I get from simply giving. And, I felt better when I gave without strings at-

try this:

What do you think makes a good friend? Think of a person who is a great friend to you and describe him or her. Write a tribute.

tached. As I let go of getting results and simply focus on the giving, true friends began popping up. When I released my expectations of what others should do to prove their loyalty and love for me, I began attracting friends. Some of them became lasting companions, while others have faded in and out of my life.

At times, this is hard for me. I am surrounded by many successful, awesome people, but not all of them want a deep and meaningful friendship with me. Some simply want to exchange business contacts, say "hello" at events and share a story or two on chance meetings. They don't want to eat a meal at my home or let me see who they are without their titles. Meanwhile, I want to rip through the layers, express my own truth and magically create the lifelong friendships *I* want. Why does this have to take *so much time?* But I'm learning that we must, instead, trust that who we are is who we should be and that the right people will come into our lives at the perfect time and in the best possible way.

Today, I am surrounded by many extraordinary, kind and genuine people. They love me for who I am, and they graciously accept (and treasure) my unconditional love in return. They are each on their own journeys through life, but our paths have crossed, and we have chosen to travel at least parts of the road together.

At the same time, I've learned that a good relationship with *me* is at the source of great friendships – and that it's actually a prerequisite for building healthy relationships with others. After all, why should someone want to get to know me, and ultimately love me, if *I* don't know and love myself?

Knowing that I can attract great people by getting to know, trust and like the greatness in me is empowering. Conversely, wishing and hoping great people will let us into their circles so that we can learn from them feels disempowering. As I continue focusing on getting to know me, I am finding the friends I'd longed for.

JASMINE: THE POETRY
OF FRIENDSHIP

A mutual friend introduced me to Jasmine, the woman I now call my sister, six years ago. This friend explained that we had a lot in common and might enjoy getting to know each other. So, we met at a coffee shop on beautiful day, bought drinks and headed outside to chat.

I had recently discovered that dominating conversations by talking about me the whole time was not leading me to the kind of friendships I wanted, and I vowed to be a better listener. So I opened myself up to hear her story – and what a story it was! She explained that she'd gotten into the life insurance business because of a fairly recent personal tragedy. At a family picnic, five of her nephews were playing in the water when the undertow swept them from the safety of the shallow shores and into serious danger. Jasmine's fiancé, Ryan, and her brother-in-law jumped in to save them. They managed to bring four boys safely back to the shore, but neither Ryan nor the fifth boy ever returned. Ryan had no life insurance, she explained, so she was left on her own with a pile of bills, their home to deal with and no financial infrastructure. She had to get back to work quickly, even though she needed more time to grieve.

Listening to her intense story, I found myself thinking, "Does my story even matter right now?" Still, I frequently wanted to interject, "But, listen to this, Jasmine." Instead, I did my best to stay focused on her.

It felt like we had just sat down when we realized an hour had passed and we both needed to go. We shared a hug, appreciated each other for the time together and rushed off to our meetings. While Jasmine's story was certainly captivating and her energy positive, I left feeling annoyed that she didn't know anything about me. Because I saw no potential for business and didn't know how this relationship could benefit me, I didn't reach out again. And neither did she.

Almost three years later, I asked Jasmine to help me form a group for young professionals in the D.C. area. She agreed, and over the next year, I grew to like and trust her, but I felt something was missing in our friendship. When she shared, it felt empty, like I was listening to a recording. Yes, she told me her intensely personal story on the day we met, but it was one she'd shared with many people (death was, after all, part of her business). I wanted to hear about things she didn't tell just anyone. I wanted to feel close to her, like I was special.

During a drive in her little Honda Civic to a networking function, I brought it up. "I really want to feel close to you," I said. "But you don't share much. You listen to all my stories, and I'm grateful, but I haven't really felt you be vulnerable with me." My heart sped up just a bit as she rolled her shoulders back and sat quietly for a few minutes. "Jasmine, I am…"

"Misti, I'm just taking it in," she said. "Give me a few minutes."

"OK." Each minute felt like an hour as I waited for her to say something, fearing the worst – that she would abandon me like so many others had.

Finally, she spoke: "You raise an important point. I understand your need to feel close to me through my vulnerability. I'm used to being the strong one, the one who holds everyone else's emotions, but I want to grow in this area. While I cannot promise it will happen overnight, I will work on sharing more with you." Then, as if reading my mind, she added, "Regardless of how much I share, you are important to me, and I'm not going away."

I felt more connected to her than ever before. While I didn't fully trust her yet, those words were more healing than I could ever fully express.

This beautiful young woman wanted to be my friend and somehow knew what I needed to hear. Jasmine kept her promise and slowly began sharing with me. I didn't even notice she was opening up until a few months later. Looking back, I think my need to feel important was already fulfilled by her words that evening, which left her free to open up at her own pace.

Later that year, Jasmine and I planned a writing trip with our friend Calvin. Jasmine would be focused on her poetry, Calvin on a book concept and website material and I on completing my first book, *From Boomers to Bloggers*. Another friend, Amanda, offered us her beach home in North Carolina. During our four-hour drive, Jasmine shared a dream she had the night before. Work had been busy for her, so she considered canceling our writing trip. But her father, whom she had recently lost to cancer, showed up in the dream and told her to stop worrying and join us.

I was only half-listening as I worked diligently in the backseat to clear my inbox. But when she started telling us about our writing trip in her dream – and began describing Amanda's house to a "T" – she had my full attention. Chills began running down my spine, because she had never been there. The more she shared, the more eerie it felt. She spoke of vibrant colors and birds everywhere. I'm not sure I could accurately describe how much Amanda loves parrots. There are parrot pictures and parrot knick-knacks or trinkets literally all over her beach home – on her furniture, walls, rugs, lamps, you name it. When I'm there, I make a point of trying to find something (*anything*) that does not have a parrot on it.

As the weekend went on, all of the things Jasmine described in her dream happened. While it was only for a brief minute (long enough for her to run inside, grab her camera and snap a photo), a beautiful rainbow graced us with its presence. And on our way home, out of nowhere, there were suddenly hundreds of thousands of birds flying around our car. If Jasmine wasn't so great, that would have really creeped me out! Instead, I decided she was clearly connected to some greater energy, and I wanted to be a part of it, whatever "it" was.

Jasmine has experienced much loss in her young life. She stood by her father's side as he took his last breath just two years after the tragic picnic, and reeled from the intense sense of loss when she learned that her best friend of 14 years committed suicide just two years after that. And now she's supporting her uncle as he undergoes chemotherapy and fights for his life.

She exemplifies such grace and optimism that she inspires those blessed enough to be part of her life. Sure, she's lost it a few times emotionally, but at the end of the day, she comes back to her center and somehow sees the gifts in each experience. And that's a task that would have been too much for Pollyanna herself if she had lived life in Jasmine's shoes. Every time she pays me a compliment about how well I'm handling something, I tell her that my strength is, in part, due to the fact that she's a brilliant mirror and that I love learning from her.

I have never met anyone loved by more people than Jasmine. Likewise, I've never met anyone she did not like. Somehow she sees beyond the layers and into the core of each person. Unlike me, she rarely finds herself triggered by anyone. No one is perfect, but Jasmine is the most perfectly imperfect person I have ever known.

When Francesca and I got married, we asked Jasmine to preside over our ceremony. We wanted someone who knew us well, who was spiritually centered and deeply kind. While I put together most of the script, Jasmine copied each piece into her own beautiful journal ("so that I can keep it with me forever," she said) and added a poem of her own:

I feel the stillness of winds
Soft touches of peacefulness upon my skin
You stand beside me
Through cloudy skies; through moonless nights
Your smiles makes every part of me feel right

Your gentle heart can see the tears
Beyond the laughter
You have found your way to settle
So naturally inside the deepest
Chambers of my heart.

You guide me through my complex fears
So lovingly, so patiently
Through rainy days; through stormy seas
Your love has lifted my soul.

To love, to live, to trust
And become the person I am
Meant to be.

You, my love, set my spirit free.

While the conversation in the car that day more than three years ago took our friendship to the next level, it is the consistency of such open and honest conversations that continues to deepen our sisterhood.

interlude
"BARE"

It's Fall, and as I watch the trees in D.C. evolve from deep green to beautiful shades of yellow, to vibrant red (some moving more quickly through this process than others) leaving a sea of yellow, green and deep pink, I can't help but think of the change that's occurring inside me.

Eventually the vast majority will be left bare, turning brown before falling to the ground. When Fall is complete, I will see the bones of the trees and will, in fact, be able to see what's beyond them. What lies beyond the trees will be ever-present and the sounds will travel easily through the air, as the leaves have fallen to make way.

I see the many shades of vibrant color, held tightly to my effervescent core that is screaming to be witnessed. I see them and I'm ready to experience my life as the magnificently beautiful leaves — you know, the ones who have guarded me my whole life. They fall to the ground and expose the core of who I really am.

I am learning to fall in love with these beautiful leaves. There are many. I know they will always be there with me, as I delve closer and closer to my inner self. I'm ready to watch a few release and fall next to me. I will enjoy their beauty from all angles.

As they fall and I begin to see myself more clearly, what will I find? As I've asked before, who am I without all the titles I have given myself? What is it, really, that I live for? What has begun to emerge is a part of my trunk whose roots I will come to know in time.

I live to feel — to feel all my emotions and witness others becoming brave enough to experience theirs. I live to love — to love all of myself and watch as others fall in love with all they are. I live to learn — to learn about myself and experience the ways so many others understand life. I live to create joy — inside myself, and then to watch as it transcends the world.

stage three
Self–Knowledge Beneath the Surface

TRANSFORMATION:
From Outward Success to Inner Security

"The individual, through prolonged psychological discipline, gives up completely all attachment to her personal limitations, idiosyncrasies, hopes and fears, no longer resists the self-annihilation that is prerequisite to rebirth in the realization of truth and so becomes ripe at last for the great at-one-ment."

JOSEPH CAMPBELL, *THE HERO WITH A THOUSAND FACES*

The veil is a powerful image in old stories and myths. Letting go of who we think we are, releasing other's expectations of us and casting off the masks we show to others, is crucial in the quest for self-knowledge. Even modern-day heroes like Batman and Wonder Woman wear masks to protect their identities.

My journey has taught me that our veils are usually protective layers we put up as a front – our "idiosyncrasies, hopes and fears, personal limitations," as Campbell puts it. But then we start to identify with them and need them to function, even though they tarnish (or mask) our view of the world. Eventually the masks we create to disguise ourselves from others become the faces that *we* see in the mirror.

This is not to say that our masks are "bad." They just *are*. They allow us to relate to others, and to some degree, even ourselves. When we label these masks "bad," we reject a part of ourselves. When we fight them, judge them or pretend they don't exist, we give them power to mask our authentic spirits. However, when we acknowledge them, and fully accept and embrace them, they dissolve, allowing our authentic spirits to surface. And if that authentic self is a big, fat liar, well, give that liar a hug and help her find her way to the honest woman she wants to be, the honest woman she is deep down. At the end of the day, just as a bride must un-veil her face to kiss her beloved, the masked hero must finally reveal his true identity to at least a chosen few in order to have real relationships.

I've learned that I can be manipulative, dishonest and selfish. I celebrate this realization because the more aware I am of these characteristics, the more I see their value. Rather than trying to hide, fade or fix them, which ultimately gives them more power, I can accept them as a strategy and come back to the present moment where such strategies are not needed. Believing that none of these things are inherently "right" or "wrong" frees me to be with all parts of my identity.

The poet Mary Oliver advocates the shedding of layers. She writes:

> *You do not have to be good.*
> *You do not have to walk on your knees*
> *for a hundred miles through the desert, repenting.*
> *You only have to let the soft animal of your body*
> *love what it loves.*

Amen, sister! It's often scary to let go; we worry what we'll actually find underneath all of those layers. It could even be a void. I continue to make that journey. And as I peel back the layers that hide my core, I continue to find … a void. All my fears about discovering I'm nothing were true. But as it turns out, that's not really a bad thing; in fact, it's liberating. Each of us is a blank canvas, and each of us is also the artist who gets to construct the masterpiece. We don't have to be anything or anybody … ever. All we really need to do is *be*.

HIDDEN TREASURE IN BALI

On my honeymoon, I came close to this experience of just being. Every-where we went in Bali, we found creativity and spirituality – as we walked down the pathways along the beach, got lost on a motorbike and traveled through a few of the small villages. It was a culture shock for sure, but my spiritual side felt more alive and full than I'd ever experienced. I did not understand what I was feeling, but I was high on it.

I loved watching the many spiritual rituals performed a minimum of three times each day. In one of my favorite rituals, participants lit incense, placed it on a sacred statue and used their hands to whip the small string of smoke toward their faces so they could breathe it in. I tried this many times and found it grounded me and helped me feel connected to everyone and everything.

During our time there, we saw many different communities performing spiritual rituals, which often blocked the road and made our drives much longer than originally intended. I'd roll down my window, poke my head out and enjoy the warm sun on my face as I witnessed the most incredible ceremonies. Fortunately, our driver, Wayne, spoke English well and helped us understand what they were chanting about and why the women were carrying big baskets of fruit on their heads. They bring those beautiful baskets of vibrantly-colored food to the temple as an offering to the Gods. Afterwards, they eat it up in celebration of the Universe.

I got a glimpse of what life could be like if I began trusting myself and the Universe a bit more. I held tightly to the freedom I felt while there by imitating what seemed to give the people of Bali peace; I created rituals. I decided to take my own spiritual awakening to another level – meditation. This required silence, both outward and inward, and silence is certainly not my specialty. But when in Rome…, right? In America, where there are television sets in practically every home, a radio in nearly every car, cell phones, text-messaging capabilities and iPods, it's almost impossible to find quiet time to reconnect with our spiritual/creative sides and just sit with ourselves for a few minutes. Of course it's *possible*; it just isn't modeled and is, therefore, rarely practiced.

While rituals and deep meditative silence initially created confusion in my typically-overactive brain, I was determined to sit with all of my feelings. And my stubbornness eventually won out over my ADD. Finally, I was able to quiet my mind long enough to recognize the truths that had been there all along, though I'd been too distracted by life to recognize them. I was using food, work and other distractions to try and satiate my hunger for words of affirmation and success, and for the feeling that I am valuable in this world. Yet, none of those things have worked, because the truth is that everything I need to feel whole is *in me*.

In Bali, I didn't feel like I was missing anything. I completely lost track of time and allowed myself to be consumed by many adventures. When I was hungry, I ate; in fact, sometimes I ate when I wasn't hungry because the food tasted so good. When I felt like going for a walk, I did. When I wanted a massage, I walked down the beach, handed over $6 and laid on a table for an hour. I had everything I needed and I was free to simply be me.

This is not to say that I fully accepted my truths right away. While it all seemed so clear during meditation and spiritual rituals, when they were over, doubt, fear and insecurities tag-teamed my new truths. And the truth that I found most valuable, the realization of my own wholeness, took the hardest hit.

During one of our many lazy, peaceful moments on the beach in Sanur, it occurred to me that I am an artist. Later, soon after arriving in Ubud, I noticed a flyer for a writers' festival. Looking at it, I realized that my art is the written word.

This realization set off inner-turmoil. Me? A writer? Aren't writers the ones who struggle through life, praying to create something good enough to get noticed and recognized? I didn't want to wear the title "starving artist." I did not want this as my truth.

But I also wanted to feel safe to share my gifts without concern about someone else being so much better, without constantly having to prove myself. In a world – my world – that seems so competitive, I felt pressure to achieve more, to be more, to be better. No, I wanted to be the best. Or, at the very least, one of the best. In my head and heart, the mantra was "beat them" rather than "be me." Anything less than the best would mean I'd missed out on something.

To my surprise and delight, while in Sanur I learned that my first book, *From Boomers to Bloggers,* was No. 2 on the *The Washington Post's* Top 10 Non-Fiction Best-Sellers list, beating out well-known books by well-known authors I respected. I celebrated for a brief moment by dancing around and sharing my news with anyone who would listen, even if they didn't understand a single word I was saying.

Minutes later, I felt empty again. So my book *had* been reported as one of the most successful by a reputable newspaper. "It's not enough" rippled through my mind as the plane landed in D.C. and there weren't a million people waiting to welcome me home and congratulate me. Maybe, just maybe, getting calls from the *Today Show* or CNN would fill this void. Perhaps if I could just surround myself with people who sang my praises, I would feel whole. I know, it sounds exceptionally egotistical and, well, it is. This sort of attention would not validate me as a person – only as an attachment to a persona that was not me, only a mask.

Slowly, it became clear – that ever-present restless sense of missing something, of not being enough, of always needing more, was the very thing preventing me from finding what I sought and being who I am. All the ego strokes in the world are nothing but veils hiding our faces from ourselves and each other. This awakening was far more useful than even the peace I found in Bali. This awareness gave me the freedom to create peace in each moment – with or without a vacation.

There's a Hindu story of a beggar who stood outside the kingdom gates day after day, asking for alms. He gradually grew thinner, begged harder and slowly wasted away. When he was finally unable to stand, he continued to beg but was never able to get enough to sustain his life. Finally, he died. The kingdom's civil servants came around to remove the body after a while. A few years later, they decided some work on the gates required excavation of the very spot on which the beggar died. Lo and behold, when they dug, they discovered a world's wealth of treasure right beneath the place where the man had stood begging his whole life. The treasure was there, right beneath him all along, but he never knew it. The story is an analogy for the human condition, philosophers say. We have the gifts, the meaning and everything else we need within us, but most of us never know it's there because we're too consumed with spending our lives begging, starving and dying to uncover it.

Back in the everyday world of business in D.C., everything in my life seems to be centered around two – maybe three – things. First, there's work. Second, there's scheduling a break from work, and finally, there's investing time and energy in developing friendships, which often end up being about work. So, really, my life is about work.

I know that as a savvy, young professional woman I'm not supposed to admit that. I'm supposed to know it's true but pretend that it's not; it makes me seem much hipper to appear more balanced. But what is balance anyway?

The definition of balance varies from person to person, and from one stage of our life's journey to the next. Sure, we can strive for whatever "balance" means to us at a given point in our lives, but obsessing over it can create more stress than not having enough of it. And while it may be a goal for many of us, none of us will have it all of the time. Stuff happens. In fact, most of us have, at some point, subconsciously unbalanced things just to have something to balance.

Besides, I *love* my work. In fact, who am I without my work? Who exists without all of those speeches about leadership and constant press for helping people see their brilliance? If I could not talk about leadership or work in any way, who would I be?

This is a question many of us have, at some point, asked ourselves. It's the question asked in the Hindu story of the beggar. My immediate reaction to this question has always been to go busy myself with work, reacting, in a way, like the beggar, who only begged harder and longer, constantly seeking for more to fill him up.

Sometimes, I feel like I have the answer and for a brief moment I know exactly who I am – without successes and titles and validation. Then, as soon as I have it, the feeling is gone, and I'm left feeling empty again. Fearing the discomfort of that void, I often turn to distractions. And when we really want to be distracted, there are just *so* many options – work, food, friends and even reality television if you're desperate. The problem is that they get in the way of getting to know ourselves, and we are back to being the hard-working beggar, oblivious to our own worth. Surely some brilliant person has created a distraction that's both fun and helps us get to know the core of who we are, right? I just haven't found it yet. For those of you thinking, "meditation," well, *I* have yet to experience that as fun!

I know from experience that taking some quiet time to tune into and sort through my feeling of emptiness will ultimately free me, but sometimes I don't even realize I've neglected myself. And, sometimes, fearing being left alone with my feelings of inadequacy, I trick myself into thinking, "If I just have enough meetings, write enough, speak enough or help enough people, I'll feel full." I keep reminding myself of the truth that don Miguel Ruiz notes: "*We know that we are pretending to be what we are not in the name of perfection.*" And a whole lot of striving goes into this illusion of perfection, which is completely out of synch with the reality of life. Perfection is only an illusion. Eventually, the pain becomes too much, and I must allow myself the quiet, reflective time my soul needs to heal and grow.

In Bali, ritual is the tool for maintaining balance, connectedness and purpose. There are rituals for all the temples (even small neighborhood temples) inviting the gods to join them in celebration. There are rituals and holy days for knowledge, science and the cycle of life (i.e., birth, death and marriage). The gods descend from their mount (Gunung Agung – sacred abode of gods and ancestors, or "heaven") to be entertained and fed. Bright colors – mostly reds and oranges – magnify the beauty of the celebration. For those who partake in these rituals, doing their part to create harmony in the world, inner balance is the natural result.

With so many rituals and such a strong connection to community, I cannot imagine how anyone's ego could get too big in Bali. Everything in the culture is about giving thanks and helping each other and the Earth. So I decided that, of all the souvenirs I'd take home with me, this lesson would be my most treasured.

SEEK PEACE AND PURSUE IT

Sure, I had rituals in D.C. They just happened to cause anxiety, fear, uncertainty, anger, frustration and a feeling of isolation. When I felt a sense of disconnect, I didn't go to the temple; I went to my computer and got to work, hoping my success would someday bring me a connection to others. But after returning from Bali, I understood that finding the inner peace that would allow me a closer connection to others meant getting closer to myself.

I began meditating and praying every morning and evening, stretching my muscles and consciously reducing the amount of restrictions I placed on my schedule. But it is a hard practice. Over time, meditation became a chore that I could hardly wait to finish, and checking e-mail on my phone once again became my first distraction of the day. Once distracted, I put myself to the side and focused on *doing*. Thoughts reinforced my actions ("This will lead to success" or "just work harder and you'll have freedom") and the hungry beggar ruled the day once more.

But I was deceiving myself. Carolyn Myss, therapist and author of *Anatomy of the Spirit*, puts it best:

> Contain your experience with the divine so that it does not escape you but rather shapes you. Be silent. Silence will help you avoid engaging in the games of competition and illusion that regularly seduce us in the outside world. Silence also helps you avoid distraction. It helps focus the busy mind – the mind that always has to be doing something, thinking something, the mind that al-

ways has to be otherwise engaged lest it become introspective and allow the soul's voice to override its own.

Often, my thoughts outshout my soul. When this happens, it takes all of my concentration to achieve short-lived silence.

In Bali, every April, the whole country observes Nyepi, a day of silence, during which work, socializing, driving, loud TV and talking, even *love-making*, are suspended. The silence is described as descending with a sense of peace so powerful you can almost touch it. How wonderful that a whole country can do something for 24 hours that most people find difficult to do for even a moment!

Myss describes the silence that radiates throughout Bali during Nyepi and radiates within those who are faithful to their practice of peace:

> [It] is a silence that you use to contain the grace you receive when you enter the Castle of your soul. This quality of silence allows you to engage in discernment. You carry this silence within you, even when you are with others. It allows you to hold your center amid the chaos of your life; it keeps you clear so that you do not do or say things you will regret or make decisions out of fear.

When I feel troubled and afraid, I know I need to get quiet and listen to myself, to pay attention to and release all the noise clogging up my brain. But it's hard enough for me to stop long enough to listen to the birds outside my window, much less the intensely negative thoughts pinging around inside my head. Yet, to this day, it is the only way I have ever found real peace. At first, it doesn't feel peaceful, and I want more than anything to just go back to my distractions. Then, gradually, with time and patience, my needs become clear.

That said, it's an ever-evolving process, one that I take moment by moment. When Francesca and I relocated to Columbia, Maryland, the change terrified me in the beginning. The day we put our house in Virginia on the market, we went to look for a place to rent in our new city, then stopped for dinner at a friend's home. At about 7:30 that night, our real estate agent called: "Congratulations, we have an offer." *Already?* While I was still terrified by the thought of the move, I was excited that we'd gotten over this first hurdle so quickly. But Francesca didn't quite see it the same way. We were losing our home.

That night, back in the house where we'd lived for three and a half years, I sat on my meditation pillow, trying to calm my thoughts. I lost it. I got up, went into Francesca's office, where she was playing a video game to de-stress, folded my arms on her desk and opened the flood gates. "I don't want to lose this home, Francesca," I sobbed. "Give me one reason why we should leave." But Francesca, who was also in a negative place, had nothing to offer. As I walked back into our master bedroom, it hit me: "I'm feeling scared because of the way I'm thinking. But what *am* I thinking?"

I grabbed my journal and began writing down all of my thoughts – without any self-censorship or consideration about "right" and "wrong." I wrote that I was afraid I'd never have a safe place to sleep again, that my business was going to fail because I was moving away from my network and that my relationship with Francesca might not make it because of the stress. It felt like all of the layers that protected and cushioned me from the world were being painfully peeled off like a bandage. Once I got it all out, I stopped to read what I had written, and I asked

> **try this:**
>
> *Create a ritual for yourself — something to either begin or end the day. It doesn't have to mean anything to anyone but you, but be clear about what that meaning is.*

myself how each thought was serving me. Then, I could see it clearly; I had let my fear make me so frantic that I was putting on darker layers of protection, painting an ugly future – one distorted and completely detached from reality.

After that journal session, I made a firm commitment to cultivate internal silence and peace, to let go of all of my preconceived notions and irrational hopes and fears so I could stay present to what is and pray for what I want. Instead of making a dramatic plea to feel safe or folding my arms and demanding reasons for the changes in my life, the only thing that really brings me peace during stressful times is genuinely and closely listening to myself, thus journaling.

That night, I slept well for the first time in almost a week. The noise can always can be quieted – once we notice and acknowledge its presence and decide we're done hurting. Sometimes it takes being in a dark place to see light. Facing the darkness brings peace; running from it only perpetuates the cycle and takes us off the hero's path.

We can go on some harrowing detours and end up far afield by running from that which frightens us. Facing the dark and bringing those "monsters" out into the light is the only way to transform them into manageable challenges, tamable beasts that teach us something about ourselves and make us stronger.

EMBRACING THE MYSTERY
OF NOT KNOWING

When I was terrified of going through the process of writing this book, I could not turn to others for answers, as I've done most of my life. The only way to work through it was to quiet the noise around me, sit with myself and really listen. By refusing to slow down and listen to ourselves, we perpetuate a lie, a self-deception that what we do is who we are. We need to stop the doing and just be with ourselves long enough to determine what we need and who we are – rather than letting anything else, including our hectic schedules, decide for us.

I always fight the calm at first. You'd think I had some strange curse that signals fierce, blood-sucking, creatures ready to eat me alive in the event that I actually stop thinking about 15 different things at once. But when

I finally get to that place where I can be comfortable with the "not knowing" (even if only in the moment), I finally unearth my most profound grace and wisdom. In the Kena Upanishads, one of the books of Hindu scripture, it says, "To know is not to know; not to know is to know." And Socrates was proclaimed the world's wisest man by an oracle because he knew one thing – that he knew nothing. If embracing the not-knowing is the way to wisdom, then I should be quite bright by now.

Now that I've given up pretending that I should know it all and am focusing instead on embracing where I really am, I get to play and have fun. I get to celebrate when I finally learn to tell a story in a way that is clearly beneficial to my audience and not just my opportunity to use a large group for a therapy session. Watching, learning and laughing are my foundations as I venture forth into unchartered territory in my career – keynote speaking.

Wouldn't it be brilliant if we were more like children, capable of approaching each new experience as though it was an exciting adventure? While I don't advocate for older people taking up skate boarding (I've seen the result of that!), I do think there's a joy that comes when we approach new challenges with the reckless abandon a six year old would. But we don't.

It's become glaringly obvious to me why *I* lost this child-like appreciation for the unknown somewhere along the way – the insecurity and fear of embarrassment that comes with so-called maturity. Said even more simply, I don't like being vulnerable. To learn something new means admitting that I don't know what I'm doing. And I'm supposed to know what I'm doing with my life by now, right?

Case in point: To hone my skills as a speaker, I decided to attend a Toastmasters meeting – a small group brought together by an international organization to allow people to practice speaking and provide feedback to one another. Simply trying to talk myself into attending my first meeting gave me visions of a schoolteacher holding up my test, with an "F" clearly written next to my name, for the whole room to see. "I'm a speaker, dang it, and I know this stuff," I assured myself as I began looking up groups in my area.

"Yeah, but what if they see that I'm not as good as I've fooled everyone into believing?" I thought. "What if they find out I get paid to speak, and then I really mess up? What if someone else in the group, maybe someone who doesn't get paid to speak, is better than me? Will everyone suddenly find out that I have *lots* of room to grow? Will I kill my career by admitting I'm not perfect?"

I caught and silenced my mind before it could run away with me. In truth, I've found that overcoming my fear of incompetence is much easier when I admit the truth – I don't know even a fraction of it all. That oracle was right about Socrates. There is wisdom (and freedom) in knowing you don't know it all. Admitting this truth is what freed me to attend my first meeting, and what a treat! Watching others in my group brilliantly express themselves through the art of speech was far more inspiring and educational than I would have ever thought. It was (and is) exactly what I need at this point in my career – a great place to mess up and to learn.

Venturing forth, like a young child might, means letting go of all our "shoulds" and recognizing that we are exactly where we're supposed to be, learning exactly what we're supposed to be learning.

During my second visit to one of the two Toastmasters groups I now attend, I spoke for two minutes on a table topic, then announced, "Man, I was nervous." When I got back to my seat, one of the best speakers in the group elbowed me and said, "Why would *you* be nervous – you just finished speaking to a group of 1,200 people at NASA." What does a person say to that? I gave him a goofy look and wrote on a piece of paper: "I'll always have room to grow *and* I've not practiced sharing *my* stories in front of a group of people. How about you mentor me?"

His face lit up, "OK, I'll help. I'm really good at telling my stories."

It felt good to admit where I am and to have this man agree to help me, rather than judge me. Freedom comes from being present to what is without needing to hide or fix anything, including our apparent lack of understanding, ability or knowledge. My experience has shown me that when we face our fears and insecurities (e.g., "I'm a professional speaker; therefore, I should already know the basics"), their power diminishes and we get to see what lies beyond it (e.g., an awesome group of people dedicated to learning the craft of public speaking and supporting – not judging – others with the same pursuit).

This inner security, cultivated by ritual and compassion for myself, has become the light that guides me through the murky pond of not-knowing. I dive deep and let the waters lift me above my fears.

interlude
" LIFTED "

The wind whips through the trees
Some leaves hold on, reluctant to release
They know this tree and
Hold a sense of pride and connection to the roots

The wind increases in strength
The force is too much
Some leaves must release
Off they go to find a new home

The leaves fly with the wind lifting and guiding
Landing for a moment
Lifted once again
Guided once more

The leaves find their new home
With time, it feels like they're old
Until, once again, the wind increases with strength
And moves us to the next best place
to be for some time

Releasing our grip
Allowing the wind to take us where it must
Trusting in the ride
Finding comfort in this new place.

stage four

*Living In and Giving Back
to the World — A Boon*

TRANSFORMATION:
From Fiasco to Fierce Kindness

"So often we try to alter circumstances to suit
ourselves, instead of letting them alter us,
which is what they are meant to do."

MOTHER MARIBEL

In *Pathways to Bliss,* Joseph Campbell asks whether, once we agree to make the hero's journey of our life, we dare to continue pushing ourselves to new horizons, accepting the mission of new adventures, onward toward either fulfillment or fiasco. But without the risk of fiasco, fulfillment isn't even a possibility.

The bliss of a life well-lived also involves the hero's achievement – something she takes back from her quest to others in the everyday world of everyday annoyances and physical needs. Don't get me wrong. I never went off for a year to meditate or to travel the world. I stayed – and continue to stay – right here in the "mess" of life, taking one thing at a time.

"The adventurer still must return with his life-transmuting trophy," says Campbell. Sometimes I have wanted to demand, "So where is this trophy!" But I've figured it out. The prize (surprise!) is the gift of love for oneself. The trophy, or "boon" as Campbell calls it, is simply the hero's calling to share what she has learned in order to "renew the community, the nation, the planet, or the ten thousand worlds."

While I won't pretend to know anything about those ten thousand worlds, I have explored the frontiers of at least one – the world of heroism. And I have found that people are heroic in many different ways. But the greatest of these (indeed the gift that lies at the heart of most other forms of heroism) is fierce kindness.

The idea of practicing kindness may seem easy, but it requires a delicate balance. My nature has always been to please others, neglecting myself to do so. In a way, that seemed easier than focusing on my own "stuff." In the past, I got angry with myself for allowing people to take advantage of me. Today, I allow myself to discover what I need and am teaching myself how to set boundaries. I've learned that when I'm not kind to myself, it's nearly impossible to be kind to others. When I have not made the time to stop and listen to my needs and taken the necessary actions for myself, it's difficult to stop and listen to the needs of others, much less do something to help. But when I have taken care of myself, I am more present and a better listener, and my kindness shines through.

This practice of fierce kindness is transforming the stories of my life into adventures, and all the people around me into heroes. But before we can instigate the unveiling of a hero in another person, we must believe there *is* a magnificent core at the heart of that person, though it may completely covered by the strategies he or she uses to feel safe. I must admit, find it difficult to see the magic of others' cores when they exclude me from their groups, are physically or verbally aggressive, or find pleasure in telling me just how much I need to grow. These people annoy me and make it very difficult for me to see their beauty.

Throughout the past few years, I have come to appreciate all people. Ironically enough, their "meanness" rarely has anything to do with me. It's when we release the burden of others' "stuff" and look for their brilliance (sometimes *really, really* intensely) that we get to see who they really are. I've always found great truth in the idea that we find what we're looking for. When we're focused on and looking for the jerkiness of a person, we find it. Likewise, when we look for gifts, for the hero beneath the layers, we see that.

Seeing the heroic qualities in another person means looking past our own expectations and loving the person who exists right there, in that moment. If there are no "right" qualities a person must embody to deserve our love, we can simply appreciate what's showing up – inside of us and them.

The minute we deem people or their actions "wrong," we lose. "Wrong" is based on past or future expectations, none of which creates peace.

While we may not always see the gift in the moment, when we look back, it's there. Everything happens for a reason and each person has a unique set of strategies for dealing with life. Some of those strategies are more tolerable than others – but they're all strategies. Love the strategies; love the core; love the person.

The people who have stuck around, seen past my outward actions and believed in me are my heroes. Here are the stories of just a few people whose compassion taught me the self-love and care I needed to exercise this kind of transformative kindness on my own life and on the lives of the people around me.

ODYSSEY

Practicing fierce kindness toward myself has led me to realize that each person is on his or her own journey. Most truly mean well and are doing the best they know how. As I consider the values and lessons my parents have taught me, I've come to a place of immense gratitude for all they are.

They've always taken a stand for what they believe in, teaching me a great deal about courage, authenticity and loyalty. And while I'm sure they didn't enjoy taking me to court for stealing, they stood next to me through all of it. And I doubt that packing up all of our belongings and hitting the road in a tiny trailer was their idea of fun. My parents were quite comfortable in their jobs. But it was likely the only thing they could think to do to help their children, none of whom were doing well in their surroundings. They figured a change of pace might make a difference – and it did.

When I was 12 years old, just out of seventh grade, my parents decided to relocate. We left our home in Commerce City, Colorado, and headed out in search of a better community and a new life for our family. They packed up me, my 13-year-old brother, Lance, and my 16-year-old sister,

Diane. My other brother, Mark, 19, stayed behind.

My dad bought an old trailer that was literally falling apart – the roof was caving in, and the inside was a disaster. It was eight by 30 feet with a very small room in the back. Dad took the old heap and crafted a home with two bunk beds in the center, two drawers and two tiny closets for me and my sister. There was a small kitchen with a sink, a stove and cabinets, and a living room area with a sofa that pulled out into a bed for Lance. Diane remembers us affectionately calling it "The Green Slime."

In no time, Dad had repaired the roof and completely remodeled the inside. It looked awesome. He has always been one of the most talented craftsmen I've known. He could fix anything and build whatever we needed. Looking back, I realize he didn't always know what he was doing, but he was always brave enough to figure it out. A small electric shock never stopped him!

So, like Odysseus on his journey to find his way back to the safety and stability of home, we set off in the newly-transformed Green Slime.

It was extremely small for a family of five. And the close quarters were made worse by my bed-wetting issue. It was bad enough when I had my own room and could close the door if it stunk. It was an entirely different experience to stink up the trailer where everyone had to sleep, eat, watch television and hang out.

Because most of us kids were born in Wisconsin and the majority of our family lived there, that was our first destination, though it was clear that my parents were hoping Dad would land a job along the way and we could settle before we got to Wisconsin.

On our journey, we stayed in campgrounds while my father looked for work. After a couple weeks without success, we'd be on the road again. Before long, we arrived in Wisconsin, where we parked the Green Slime in my aunt's driveway for two or three weeks while my parents were job hunting – unsuccessfully. As independent as all of the strong women of myth and legend, my mother preferred raising her children and living her life on her own terms, without what she would call the "drama of family." So, she seemed happy when we were on the road again, headed back toward Colorado.

Almost as quickly as we reentered Colorado, we ran out of money. There was a lake my parents used to take us to on summer weekends where it cost very little, if anything, to camp. We pulled the trailer a safe distance from the water, set up our home for the next several weeks and lived by our strength and wits. Just like when we camped for fun, we used the bathroom outdoors and bathed in the lake. While the lake always had a layer of grime on top, cloudy water the color of seaweed and a bottom so slippery that we couldn't stand up for long, at least we got to use shampoo!

My parents got new jobs. They didn't pay much, but it was enough to get us a modular home in a very small town called Crook, Colorado. We lived there for a year, barely able to afford food and clothing. My mother highly disliked not being able to flood us with present for the holidays. So, in her quest to find a better life for her family, she got her old job back in Commerce City and, after months of her commuting and staying with a friend during the week, we all loaded back into the Green Slime for another summer.

Just before summer ended, we found a bigger trailer and a piece of land in another small town about 30 miles north of Denver called Gilcrest. To afford it, my father devised a brilliant and heroically resourceful plan.

My parents went to a nearby auction and bought two very old, beat-up, uninhabitable trailers, and my family worked together to tear them apart. We began by ripping off the aluminum siding, which my father turned over for cash. Next, we tore all of the copper wire out of the trailer, brought it to our campsite and burned it. We all loved watching the pretty colors that came off the wires as the plastic burned away, leaving the wire clean and therefore more valuable for resale. Once the walls and ceiling were removed, my parents took the trailers to the same auction and sold them as flatbeds.

While I highly disliked the hard work that went into tearing those trailers apart, it was better than sitting around, bored out of our minds, and within weeks we had the money to buy our new home. With $5,000 in hand, my father negotiated a deal with the owner of an older, completely trashed, but still habitable trailer. The caveat? We got it "as is" and agreed to clean the lot the trailer had been sitting on – which entailed more hard work, as the former renters had not minded living in filth. It took us a couple weeks to empty out that trailer, clean the lot and find a trailer park with an open lot. My father found the perfect piece of land – the biggest lot in a park just outside Gilcrest. It was far enough from the city to keep us children out of trouble, but close enough for Mom to drive to Commerce City for work.

This family odyssey set the tone for my life. Later, I would have to once again strike out into the unknown – this time in search of a meaningful career. Like my parents wanted more for their children, I want more for myself and the little girl within me. Often, I have had to build from scratch and to scrap a couple of worn-out ideas for a new one in which I could live and breathe.

A TALE OF TWO MENTORS

⚜

It was during high school in Gilcrest, and then in early college, that I learned the transformative power of belief. Figures of authority, with whom I'd normally be in conflict, noticed qualities in me of which I wasn't even aware.

I will always remember my first meeting with the principal at Valley High. Principal Wiser sat behind his big wooden desk, hands folded together as though praying (which he probably was ... praying that my mother would stop talking soon). She shared all the challenges I'd experienced and the special programs I'd been enrolled in over the past two years. She wanted him to fully understand our situation so he could place me into the most appropriate classes. Meanwhile, I shrank in my seat, joined Principal Wiser in silent prayer and waited for him to explain what I would need to do that was different from all of the other students. To my absolute surprise, he calmly said, "Mrs. Burmeister, I think your daughter is quite normal and will get along just fine in our regular classes."

I could tell Principal Wiser had heard it all, so he must have known something that neither my mom nor I knew. The man I'd eventually call a hero gave me hope for the first time that I might be normal. If he thought I would do well in his school, then I most certainly would. This was my first lesson in the power of words. His words, his confidence in me, changed my life that day.

I graduated in the percentage of the class that made the top part impressive. If my homework didn't fold up and fit into my back pocket, I didn't take it home. But I did become a three-time state champion in track and was named "Student Athlete of the Year" by the *Greeley Tribune*, our local newspaper. That helped me get my foot in door at the University of Northern Colorado, where they had the Challenge Program, which offered probationary enrollment for underperforming high-school students now ready to prove their academic abilities.

try this:

Name one or two mentors who have had the greatest impact on your life. What specifically did they do to help you excel? What types of mentoring skills do you possess? Name one or two people in your life right now you could mentor to make a positive impact in their life/lives.

The Challenge Program classes were taught by some of the school's most patient and caring teachers. It was located inside the Arts & Sciences Advising Center, which gave us a generous and dedicated support staff to help us craft our four-year-plans and navigate the campus and school system. During my first semester, I spent hours in the center every week. Before long, it became a second home for me. Pamela, the woman in charge of the center, and Cynthia, an academic advisor, took a particular interest in me and offered me a job advising incoming Challenge Program students. It

paid in academic credits rather than cash, but I was honored and immediately accepted.

First, I had to take a "how to" course taught by Cynthia, a calm, generous, loving woman with an incredible ability to listen authentically. Her
office ultimately became a safe place for me to share my life. The magic of
Cynthia was in her ability to listen without judgment or pretense. She believed in me and always trusted that I would find my own answers. Whatever I was going through at any particular time in my life was always perfect
in Cynthia's eyes, which made it all more palatable for me. When I thought
I was crazy for whatever emotion I was experiencing, Cynthia would help
me see the importance of those feelings. "It makes sense that you feel that
way," she told me many times. She was the first person to show me how
to express myself in a calm, self-nurturing and honest way. With her, I felt
safe to be all of myself without fear of rejection. Much like Linda, the spe-
cial-education teacher who refused to give up on me in grade school, Cynthia loved me without condition, and we continue to check in via
telephone from time to time.

Looking back, I can see that she gave me one of the first hints that there
could be something heroic and lovely beneath all my complicated layers.
I never expected her to fix anything, but I could always create my own answers in her presence. Life can be hard, so it's nice when someone shows
up to greet us where we are, hold our hands, listen and tell us they believe
in us. When someone provides us with a blank slate (a loving mirror in
which we can see ourselves clearly), it's easier to see our own truths and feel
empowered to make the best choices.

Providing this type of support is not always easy. Often, as I listen to
people share their pain, I immediately want to reciprocate by sharing my
own experiences. In doing so, I take the attention off of them and bring it
back to me. Over time I've gotten better at listening without interruption
and sharing what makes sense only after people have the chance to experience their feelings. When they're stuck, I imitate Cynthia and probe fur-

ther, allowing them to uncover their own answers.

I try to remember this lesson every time I'm tempted to "fix" someone, especially my family members. Trying to fix someone assumes he or she is broken, which isn't the least bit empowering or helpful. Who am I to determine whether anyone is broken? But focusing on what's amazing about that person just may help an individual feel whole again.

The greatest and most painful struggles in my life have also been the moments when I grew the most. Those experiences did not become opportunities for growth because someone else swooped in to give me the answers. As I struggled through my own challenges, the people who helped me the most along my journey were those, like Principal Wiser and Cynthia, who listened to my stories without trying to hide, fade or fix any of it. They heard the meaning behind my words and saw beneath my surface. Their kindness enabled me to uncover a better, stronger, wiser and happier person deep down, one who was there all along but needed someone else to recognize her.

COLLEGE ALGEBRA

Though it may seem like small potatoes compared with some of the major tragedies and challenges most of us face in our lives, College Algebra was a defining moment for me, one of those big hurdles that enabled me to dig deep and discover stores of hidden strength and stamina. I'd barely passed Algebra-I in high school and never bothered to take any other math courses.

As I sat through my first class, I suddenly realized why all my advisors had encouraged me to go to the local community college and get the basics. My eyes were open. I was hearing the teacher's words and even taking some notes (mostly because that's what the other students were doing) but wasn't sure she was even speaking English. "Integer, whole number, pie (don't you eat those?), squared (the shape of a box, right?), etc." I was beside myself.

After class I waited until everyone left to approach another would-be hero, my teacher, Sarah. I began by asking what some of the words meant. She immediately asked about my math placement test results. When I told her, she said, "You need to go to the community college and take the lowest level. You have no foundation for this class."

As she gathered her books to leave, I asked, "Sarah, are you a teacher?"

"Yes," she said, slowing her packing process – as though she was thinking too hard to pay attention to what she was doing.

"You're a teacher, Sarah, and I'm a student, so will you teach me?" After a bit of back and forth, she realized I wasn't going to give up. She told me that her office hours were right after class every day for two hours and that she fully expected me there the entire time. I thanked her and promised I would stay committed.

She started by teaching me the process for remembering multiplication tables and gave me one weekend to learn them. I did as she asked. In fact, I did exactly what she told me to do for the entire semester and miraculously out-performed all her other students. Sarah taught me to support people who need someone to believe in them – even when their success seems unlikely. Agreeing to help me was like her saying, "If *you* believe you can do it, I believe it too." Her commitment wasn't to my grade; it was to supporting someone with a goal.

> **try this:**
>
> *When have you been a dreamer? When have you been a hero? Journal about the dreamers who have inspired you and the heroes who have helped someone else realize a dream.*

I don't know what I would have done if Sarah hadn't taken on the challenge. Her gift to me was not the math lessons (heck, I've managed to forget most of it already), but rather, courage for life. Now, when I meet someone trying to do the seemingly impossible, I look for his or her conviction and offer my support. Dreamers need heroes, and heroes need dreamers. Without knowing it, they seek each other and the Universe often brings them together, uniting like minds and kindred hearts.

COMING OUT AND COMING HOME

The surprising consequences of our leaps of faith often reveal the core of another person. Hidden heroes sometimes just need the right opportunity to emerge, and what feels life-threatening at the moment becomes a life-altering gift. As I learned about myself, it was often a challenge to share what I uncovered with those closest to me. Such was the case with my sexuality. I feared that coming out to my parents would be the end of the world as I knew it. And it was, just not in the way I thought.

It was the winter of 1997, and for months, I'd spent very little time at home. At the time, the only place I knew to meet other gay people was a night club in Fort Collins, Colorado (about an hour from our home). A group of friends and I went there every Friday and Saturday night, and sometimes we gathered at one of their houses to hang out during the week.

Big-city night-life was a much needed outlet for my newfound sexuality, but the late hours were exhausting. And so was the secrecy. I wanted to share my life with my family, so it was time to come out to my parents – a prospect that terrified me. Did I dare? They had never been discreet about their distaste for the homosexual community; I'd heard them use the words "faggot" and "dyke" countless times. I knew they might reject me, but it had to be done.

It was the holiday season, so my siblings were home. Just before I headed home, I called. "Mom, I'm on my way and I need you to get rid of everyone so I can talk to you and Dad alone." She agreed to send them out for a Christmas tree, which would be give us about an hour, give or take 20 minutes, for our conversation.

The whole way home I was rehearsed what, specifically, I would say. Memories of my mother muttering "dyke" under her breath as we walked past masculine-looking women with short hair tortured me – as did the horror stories I'd heard from friends who'd come out to their parents.

As I approached my exit off Highway 85, I wanted to walk in there and say, "Just kidding. Everything is fine." But I knew they wouldn't buy that. Instead, I decided to tell them I was bisexual, so they'd think there was still hope for me and be less upset.

I parked my car in our gravel driveway, took a deep breath and willed myself to go inside. My mother was sitting in her usual spot, at the far end of the couch nearest the door, with her arms crossed. My father was standing (in all my life, I have only a few memories of him actually sitting). My heart beating a thousand miles an hour, I tossed my stuff on the floor and made my way to the chair directly across from them. The television was turned off, which signaled they were ready to listen. I would have much preferred it playing at full volume, drowning out my internal monologue, which went something like this: "They'll make me pack my stuff and leave. They'll call me ugly names and exclude me from the family, and, worst of all, they'll think there's something horribly wrong with me."

I tried to begin but could only muster up tears. After several minutes of sobbing, I finally managed to say, "I'm bisexual."

"That's *it?*" my father responded, looking relieved. What did he mean?! I was sharing my deepest secret, and he didn't seem to care one iota.

Realizing my mother hadn't said anything, I demanded, "Mother?" But she was staring off into space, seeming puzzled.

"We thought you were dropping out of college," explained my father.

I was too wrapped up in the emotion of my truth to process his meaning. "What? No, Dad. I like college," I assured him. "Mom, say something, please."

"Fine," she said. "But you're not bisexual, Misti. You're gay. And I don't care who you choose to have sex with. I care that you're happy and a good person."

I was confused. I paused to think about what she had been pondering; she was thinking about the way I was with boys my whole life. She was suddenly realizing that I never had much of an interest in them beyond friendship. I *had* boyfriends in high school. In fact, I dated one boy for two years and only kissed him one time. In truth, he was my best friend, who bought into the story that I wanted to wait until marriage. The thought of kissing him nauseated me, but I enjoyed his company and was grateful to have a "boyfriend" in high school; it was quite healthy for my self-esteem. "That actually seems more right, Mom," I conceded.

Much to my surprise, my parents didn't seem troubled by this new information. Mom explained that a "dyke" is a butchy lesbian, which is "disgusting." And the idea of two men having sex grossed them out. But I was a feminine lesbian, which was OK. Whatever! Over time, I came to realize that though they use ugly words to describe people of different cultural backgrounds, they always help *individuals* in need, regardless of their differences. Their ability to see beyond their own labels when faced with real people, not a faceless group, makes them heroic.

With that behind us, we turned on *Wheel of Fortune*. My father pointed to Vanna White. "Think she's hot, Misti?" he asked. He accepted me! I smiled, said she was OK and waited excitedly for another good-looking woman to come on so I could point out the type of girl I found attractive.

Soon, my siblings returned, and I shared my "news" with them. A single mother with a two year old and little support, Diane wasn't very interested in my sexuality. Lance was convinced I was simply "going through a phase" but he was kind and supportive.

A few weeks later, I brought home a girl I was dating. She looked like the women my mother called "dykes," so I worried Mom would dislike her. To my surprise, she was kind and inviting, though she later made it clear that this particular girl wasn't good enough for me. My mom, her strong and determined spirit showing again, had clearly created a vision for *my* love life and that girl would not do.

I was just happy that I could be so open with my parents, the people I trusted most. Their opinion mattered to me deeply. Over the following months, I brought home lots of girls so Mom could help me weed them out. In fact, I probably brought home more than she would have liked –

though, in truth, she didn't meet *all* the girls I went out with in that first year. (What can I say? I always have been an overachiever when starting something new. When that closet door was open, I was bolted through it at full speed.) I trusted Mom's opinion and let several girls go because they did not pass her inspection. A year or so later, I began dating my first real love, Natalie. While my mother didn't really like her, she was feminine, and I liked her a lot. So, as with all my serious relationships going forward, Mom tolerated Natalie and said very little to me about her distaste.

My two serious relationships before Francesca brought lots of discomfort and conflict, which is probably why Mom did not like them. My parents knew I had to come to terms with the kind of relationship I was looking for, so, for the most part, they kept their opinions to themselves. Their gift of acceptance was strong enough to help me make my own decisions.

A few years after I moved to D.C., my parents came to visit. At the time, Francesca and I were only friends (but best friends), and I invited her over to meet them. Minutes after she left, my mom asked if she was gay. I said she was. "Why aren't you dating *her*?" she demanded.

"She's just not right for me, Mom."

"That's the stupidest thing I've ever heard. She's perfect for you."

In truth, Francesca and I always had an attraction but never the right timing. Two months later, we found the right time. Five years later, when we got married, my parents proudly walked me down the aisle on a crowded beach in Lewes, Delaware. They bought necklaces for each of us and a set of cookware as a wedding gift. My mother even keeps our wedding photo proudly displayed on her desk. If any curious co-worker asks about it, she always says, "She never asked me to be gay. Why would I ask her to be anything other than what's right for her?" God, I love that woman!

While my siblings, all straight, sometimes have a hard time understanding my lifestyle (I don't have children, nor do I live in a small town), they embrace me for who I am. Recognizing the blessing and beauty of my family is one of the most powerful lessons I have learned on this journey – and one of the most healing.

WRITING A PATH TO COMPASSION

In *Kitchen Table Wisdom,* Rachel Naomi Remen writes, "Everybody has a story . . . we may need to listen to one another's stories again . . . all real stories are true." This, she says, is why she wrote her wonderful book of short essays. While it took time (and a little struggling) for me to realize that I am a writer, I know exactly *why* I write – because I recognize the sacred in everyone's story and know that words have more healing power than any medication I've ever taken.

Even as a teenager, I understood the power of words to inspire and to empower. I posted quotes all over my bedroom walls – some sayings I created (like "When I'm not training, someone, somewhere else is, and when I meet them, they will win"), as well as words of inspiration from great thinkers like Seneca, who said, "It is not because things are difficult that we do not dare. It is because we do not dare that things are difficult." To this day, I regularly gather quotes and post them all over my home. I believe language creates reality, and words have helped me find peace over and over.

That said, it was a long leap from collecting quotes to writing a book. Sometimes we need other people to recognize and encourage our heroic talents before we can see them. I consider the people who helped me develop my writing to be among the most important guides on my path.

Ms. Preston, my high-school English teacher, seemed to enjoy punishing us with constant reading and writing assignments, which never fit into my back pocket and, therefore, rarely made it home for completion. While I tried to avoid her, I always seemed to attract her attention with my loud voice and sometimes-obnoxious behavior.

One day, I showed up late for class without my assignment (again), and Ms. Preston asked me to stay after the bell. "Misti, if I could just insert a wire from your mouth to your fingers, we'd have a great writer," she told me.

I was expecting some cruel and unusual punishment for my tardiness and uncompleted work; instead, she got me thinking. Could I really be a good writer? I mean, I *do* talk a lot. What if I sat down and just talked through writing? I was inspired. Soon after that conversation, I began visualizing myself as a writer. With this newfound vision, I started spending a lot of time in front of my computer, trying to think of what I would *say* as a response to her writing assignments so that I could capture it on paper. Before long, I found some flow to my writing and became quite decent at it – for the high-school level.

A graduate program, however, required a whole new level of writing. The first semester of my master's program, I had a Communication professor, Dr. Prestridge, who insisted that our writing be "tight, concise and precise." He gave us a stack of journal articles an inch thick about the theory of communication and told us to read them and write a one-page synopsis – due in one week. He quickly became the devil I despised. When my first grade came back and it was six out of 10, I immediately made my way to his office. "Why such a low grade, Dr. Prestridge?" I insisted.

He simply said, "Tighten it up, Misti."

I didn't know what that meant, but I agreed to try and left his office convinced I would do significantly better next time. Two weeks later I got my second grade – seven out of 10. Better, yes, but I'm a perfectionist, and this irritated me. I'd spent so much time "tightening it up." In Dr. Prestridge's office later that day, I interrogated him, "What's the deal? I spent so much time working to make that paper perfect."

"Tighten it up, Misti," he responded again. I wasn't about to let him off the hook so easily this time. I wanted to smack him for being so evasive, but instead I asked him to elaborate. "Use fewer words to articulate the same point," he said calmly, clearly not the least bit bothered by my anxiety.

I left his office, read the next set of articles that day and began crafting my synopsis. Two days later, I was back in his office. "I want to get this one right before I hand it in," I told him. "Will you please review and add any thoughts about tightening?"

My stomach cringed as he leaned over the desk and began making the paper bleed with his cursed red pen. He motioned for me to take a seat next to him, and together we reviewed his comments. He also urged me to start including my opinions, rather than purely regurgitating the content I read. I listened intently, thanked him for his help, walked to the computer lab down the hall, inserted my floppy disc and began working on it right away.

When I approached his office the following day, the expression on his face (the one that said, "You again?") made it obvious that my enthusiasm was starting to try his patience. But he marked up my paper and reemphasized that I should spend some time considering what *I* think and understand from the reading, and not just paraphrase. Back to the computer lab I went, floppy disk in hand, ready for Take 3.

The next day, Dr. Prestridge didn't seem surprised to see me. This time he made fewer edits, which was a relief. Whether that was because my writing had improved or he was just tired of seeing me was irrelevant. Two weeks later, I got my paper back with a nine out of 10.

After class, I caught him in the hallway and asked, "Why did I miss a point?" (I know, I know. I was maybe a tad over-the-top!)

"It wasn't perfect," he said and continued walking. After that day, I made a pact with myself to get a perfect score. I spent the same amount of time in his office the following three weeks. Eventually, I could sense what he would say. My grade fluctuated between nine and 10 throughout the remainder of the semester. By the time I graduated with my master's degree, I had a solid foundation. To this day, I use the skills he patiently taught me.

The guy I once despised became a hero. He was unbelievably patient with me. In fact, he probably qualifies for sainthood for not running when I approached his office door for the umpteenth time). But more importantly, he helped me hone and sharpen the tool that would enable me to honor the heroes of my life in this book.

If I could pick the one skill every person should master (either in school or through practice), it would be writing. Whether you enjoy it or not, writing is a powerful tool. The ability or inability to communicate effectively can elevate our self-esteem or destroy it, get us the jobs we've always wanted or cause us to lose out on opportunities, help us gain and retain exceptional friends and stellar team members or isolate us from others. Words seem so simple and, to many, unnecessary; yet, they are a powerful way to communicate who we are, what we think and how we feel. They allow us to bond with others – by communicating a shared belief or interest, or by expressing that we care.

The *written* word strengthens all other forms of communication. It helps us to discover what we think, before we act. And it makes our actions more meaningful and consistent. The more I write, the better speaker I become. Clearly understanding and articulating my thoughts about my subject matter allows me to communicate them more effectively to others.

What's more, writing about my journey is helping me uncover *me*. Without the ability to get all my thoughts organized on paper, where I can make sense of them, they would be racing around inside my head all the time, slowly driving me mad (or madd*er*, depending on who you ask). My

> **try this:**
> *Write about a difficult moment in your life. Use poetry, or just write it straight and clear. Listen for your voice and attend to the healing power that comes from telling your story in your own words.*

brain likes to make a *big* deal out of small things; writing frees me to focus on reality, which is always much kinder than the stories I make up. When I write, my own answers appear.

Words are a mirror in which I have become familiar with my true self – and the mirror I now shine on those around me as I share the trophy I discovered on my journey with everyone who will listen.

interlude
"LET GO OF THE TRYING"

Be who you are
The world is waiting

Lean into yourself
It is safe here

Quiet the noise
Find this moment
Be in it
See yourself
Breathe

Breathe in your greatness
Breathe out "trying"
Be with yourself

In this moment
Allow the rest to fall away.

stage five
Heroes, Heroes Everywhere!

TRANSFORMATION:
From Ordinary People to Heroes

"In the end, though, maybe we must all give
up trying to pay back the people in this world
who sustain our lives. In the end, maybe it's wiser
to surrender before the miraculous scope of human
generosity and to just keep saying thank you,
forever and sincerely, for as long as we have voices."

ELIZABETH GILBERT, *EAT, PRAY, LOVE*

This book has taken me down a blessed path – an outer-inner-outer journey with concentric transformations, which I have described in the separate stages of my hero's journey. I began by trying to reframe the idea of heroes. When I looked out at the world with eyes focused on seeing the heroic qualities in others, I started to see myself in a new light. Turning that outward sight into insight, I began the long process of uncovering my true self, both in the face of the little girl and the hidden hero within me. With this newfound discovery, I traveled out of myself once again, into the world, where everything was completely new; it felt like emerging from a cave to see the sun for the first time, or coming out of a movie theater to find that rain has washed everything until it sparkles. Everyday people shone more brightly too. In these final pages, I will attempt to describe this shimmering world of ordinary, heroic faces.

EVERYDAY HEROES

I have Doug, an exceptional man and thriving real estate agent/investor, to thank for revolutionizing my idea of heroes and, consequently, changing my life. I always thought of a hero as someone who acts in extraordinary ways – a notion reinforced by the media. I considered them super-human and somehow absolutely perfect. So, if I hailed someone like Oprah or Zig Ziglar as my hero, then I would be admitting that I'm not capable of doing the magical things they have done. And then what good am I?

All these misconceptions dissolved when, while moderating a panel of successful CEOs, I asked Doug, "If you could offer any advice to our audience, what would it be?"

He responded, "It's important to keep growing, to surround yourself with people who push you outside your comfort zone. Everywhere I go, I look for the gifts in the people I meet. I go to conferences where the most successful investors speak. I find their bios on the *Forbes* website, print them off, read them carefully and keep them with me. When people ask about the file filled with the bios of my heroes, I say, 'Those are my buds, you know, my close friends.'"

Of course, the audience erupted with laughter and, at the same time, I could feel the inspiration in the air. I was both terrified by and curious about this notion. I'd never thought about heroes like this before. He began with memories of the people he considered heroes as a child, and as I listened, I felt cheated. Naturally, I did a lightning-quick search of my childhood and tried to recall a time when I envisioned myself, as Doug put it, "saying 'Jordan' as I tossed the ball toward the hoop." I could not, and still cannot, recall such heroes. What I do remember is praying to get through the day; everything in my life was about survival.

Then, he described the importance of having heroes as adults. Suddenly I felt this sense of freedom – like I didn't miss the boat. I could still have heroes. This wasn't, as I'd always believed, something only children – or weak people – could need or have. I didn't have to know everything and always *be* the hero. I could look up to someone and allow that person to grace my life with his or her gifts.

As I listened to Doug, it occurred to me that maybe heroes are like role models – people I can watch, learn from and use to help me grow personally and professionally. Doug gave me a precious gift — the understanding that it's OK to have heroes and, even more importantly, how doing so removes my feelings of isolation and creates a real sense of belonging. So, who are my heroes? It's quite simple, really. Those who, regardless of their titles or successes, choose to face their fears, share their vulnerability, take a stand for what they believe, show compassion for themselves and others, and create hope in our world. People like Doug.

I'm realizing just how many heroes I've been blessed to know and learning to appreciate them as the Universe brings them into my life. As I've begun to see the people around me — both from my past and present — through a different lens, to look for the gifts those in my life have given me rather than just the hurt, I'm realizing that I've been surrounded by unlikely heroes all along — hidden in plain sight.

DIANE: MY SISTER, MY HERO

For many, it is hardest to truly see those closest to us as heroes. When we look at our parents and siblings, the mess of old hurts and disappointments blocks our vision and makes it hard to see their heroic qualities. My vision of my family is often gummed up like a dirty mirror. But as I unearth my inner hero, I see them in a new light.

Siblings, perhaps, present the greatest challenge when it comes to seeing the hero within, because siblings are typically very different people thrown together by fate for the better part of their early lives and told not to kill one another, and to even try to *like* one another. My sister and I managed to not kill each other (though not for lack of attempts) and, on rare occasions, like each other.

And, as often happens when we no longer have to live under the same roof with our childhood rivals, the equation flipped as we matured, and now the moments of friendship usually outweigh the moments of rage that only those who share our DNA can evoke.

Diane and I have grown up a lot since the days of hand-to-hand combat in our shared bedroom. Our relationship is still a complex one, as most relationships are, because we are still two very different people. We may as well speak different languages considering the challenges we have with communication and understanding one another. But we're starting to find some common ground. And I'm learning to look past the hurt and the dynamics of sibling drama to see my sister for the hero she is.

For a long time, I felt Diane didn't provide the type of support sisters were "supposed" to provide. But while she doesn't always support me the way *I* need to be supported, she's always there for me. When I first started my company, she did my bookkeeping for the first two years – without pay.

Almost a year ago, I called her to check in. Instead of her trademark response, "I'm just peachy," she responded for the first time with, "I've been better." That was a *very* bad sign.

"What is it, sis?" I asked.

"I can't talk about it right now," she said, her tone so fearful that it scared me.

"Is everything OK?"

"Not really, but I can't talk about it right now. I need to go."

"Is it your health?" No. "Your family's health?"

"Could be. Gotta go," she said and hung up.

My gut told me to call my 14-year-old nephew. My voice shook as I asked, "What's up, Carter?"

"Nothing, just watching some TV. Did you talk to my mom?"

"Yes, and it seems like something is wrong, but she wouldn't tell me. What's up?"

Carter explained that he had begun cutting himself. His casual tone made my heart sink and my stomach knot up. I knew enough about cutting to know that people do it to deal with pain and feel some sense of control. I spent the next several minutes trying to get more information out of him, but he was done sharing.

Diane clearly didn't want to talk about this, so I tried hard to wait for her to bring it up. But after two or three days, I told her that Carter let me in on the secret. She seemed relieved to know that someone, besides her and her husband, knew about it. Over the next few weeks, she shared many of her fears, including the most recurring – that she was a bad mother.

After some time and research, Diane was able to see and accept the "gift wrapped in crap," as my therapist would say. Though talking about emotions has never been of interest to Diane, she began opening up, slowly. "I like the way I am," she argued with me at one point. But she admitted along the way that she wanted to grow from this experience, so overcoming her own resistance and trying new ways of being propelled her forward.

Diane wasn't just dedicated; she also got creative. When Carter was suspended from school for two days, she didn't want to leave him at home playing games and watching movies all day, so she volunteered him to work at a homeless shelter for the day. That stroke of mothering genius was just what Carter needed. He loved volunteering and asked to do it more often. Diane researched other nonprofits and found one for handicapped children that had a full week of events scheduled the same week as Carter's spring break. Instead of spending his time goofing around with his friends like most teenagers, he *chose* to help out – and loved it.

None of this would have happened if my sister had done what many parents do – look the other way and hope the problems will magically disappear. She has even organized a group for parents in the community to come together and help each other navigate parenthood. While I'm certain her journey will include many more learning opportunities along the way, she has proven that she's up to the challenge and that she wants to learn and grow as a person and as a parent. I'm completely inspired by the way she has handled one of the most difficult things a parent can experience. No, she didn't (and still doesn't) know exactly what's she's doing. Neither life nor children come with instruction manuals, not for any of us. But she's stepping out of her comfort zone and trying new things. For this, she is a hero.

Amazingly enough, despite our antagonistic moments (and while they are rarer now, we still have our moments), my sister recognized a hero in me many years ago. When I was in high school, doing my best to be a track and field superstar, she wrote a poem describing some of my heroic qualities, ones I am just now discovering in myself, and seeing in her and others:

Admiration: Dedication
Much like mountains,
She keeps reaching new peaks,
Like the water in a river bed bursts over every rock,
She overcomes each stepping stone,
In contrast to a tall evergreen tree drooping with snow,
We know she will spring back,
Because of her overwhelming dedication,
We know there will always be another season.
She, nature; Is my Sister.
I admire her dedication to all she does.

Misti ~ You have the ability to create your own mountains
And leap over them;
The ability to design your own rivers
And swim in them;
The ability to plant new trees
And cut them down to plant bigger ones.
Misti ~ I have big dreams and hopes for you,
As I know you have the ability to live these dreams.

A HEROIC INHERITANCE:
'TIS EASIER TO GIVE THAN TO RECIEVE

My parents have performed feats of heroism all of my life that I can now recognize and celebrate. My mother cheered me on at every track meet, despite working a full-time job. And while he didn't say much, my father supported me in very specific ways, even defying the weather when necessary.

Many times in Colorado, the winds got so strong that it felt like a tornado was coming to take our trailer away. When the wind blew really hard, our exterior walls would begin swaying, often waking me. I'd lie there envisioning a giant, black funnel pulling the wall off the trailer and then sucking me out, smashing my head against the flying debris and throwing me into buildings.

I could never get back to sleep until my father confirmed we were safe. I would knock on my parent's bedroom door, crack it open and call quietly for him, praying I didn't wake my mother. Dad would get up, go outside, light a cigarette and scan the black sky for tornados. When he finished his cigarette, he would come back inside and give me the all-clear. As if he could see a tornado in pitch dark! But it made me feel better, and I'd soon find my way back to sleep.

It wasn't just our family that my father watched over. He loved stopping to help anyone whose car broke down along the highway. Often, the folks needing help were of a different ethnic background and rarely spoke English.

My father would get out of the car, walk over to theirs and say a few basic words in Spanish: "*Hola, que pasa?*" After the initial "hello's," they'd point at the problem, and my father would help fix it. Sometimes this took 10 minutes, other times a couple hours. If they needed a part, my father would get it. Rarely did he leave someone without a running engine.

When they tried to give him a few dollars, he wouldn't accept. Instead, he'd mentioned something about "cerveza" and point in the direction of our house. Sometimes these guys would find our home and stop by with a case of beer. My father and the stranger would each have one, and while I doubt they understood much of what each other said, the deeper feeling of gratitude and camaraderie was what I remember most.

While my father's desire to stop and help didn't always fit into my mother's tight schedule, they always managed to work out the details. She wasn't always fond of this quality in my father but she understood.

To this day, I find those times fascinating, especially in the context of the words they used to describe the same people they stopped to help. It was as if their differences no longer mattered when there was a clear need. Interestingly, every time I've had car trouble, someone stopped to help.

Whenever I get the chance to help another person, I instantly remember when we, as a family, made other people's challenges our opportunity to help. All my siblings have adopted this quality of authentic generosity. It's just the Burmeister way – a heroic legacy passed down from our parents.

CRAIG: LEARNING TO
TRUST IN THE UNSEEN

By being open to astonishing generosity, I found another hero who blessed my life and gave me the modern equivalent of wings – wheels.

It was a rainy day in late November 2004, and I was driving my little Ford pick-up truck to my best friend Francesca's home. She'd agreed to drive me to the airport for a holiday visit with my family. While our homes were only 15 miles apart, I gave myself an hour, hoping traffic would be in my favor. It was bumper to bumper headed into the city, as morning commuters made their way to D.C. Fortunately, I was headed away from the city, so my side of the road was clear. "Sucks for *those* people," I thought, looking at the gridlock. My drive would be a breeze.

Off in the distance, I noticed an SUV pull half-way across the highway into the median about 400 feet in front of me, trying to ease his way into traffic. Then, to my horror, he put his car in reverse and froze in my lane.

I waved my hands, motioning for him to get out of the way. The minute I touched my brakes, they locked. I slid toward him at 50 miles-per-hour. It was only seconds until the impact, but it felt like long, drawn-out minutes. I remember the panicked look on his face as my truck smashed into the side of his vehicle. "This can't be real," I remember thinking as I finally came to a stop in the middle of the road.

It was. And what's worse, the other driver had no driver's license or car insurance, and the car wasn't even registered. And because my truck wasn't worth much, I knew what I'd get from my insurance company would be minimal. My truck wasn't fancy, but it was paid for. And where was I going to get the money for a monthly car payment?

As I watched the tow-truck driver load the hunk of metal that had been my only mode of transportation, my mind wandered to a true story I'd heard recently: A warehouse owner watched his property burn to the ground one night. As the firefighters tried to stop the blaze, one of his employees asked what they were going to do. "Rebuild," said the owner in a calm, trusting voice. "This place was clearly meant to be rebuilt, and together we'll get it done."

The story inspired me when I heard it, and made me feel a little better now. I raced to find some silver lining (or at least a good life lesson) in this frustrating experience. That warehouse owner clearly trusted in something, but I had a total of one close friend at the time and no job – and now, no way to get to job interviews. The glass looked *at least* half empty from where I stood.

During my week in Colorado, my body ached from the impact, and the uncertainty of my independence in D.C. weighed heavily on my mind. But while I was worrying, one of my massage clients, Craig, heard about what happened. He immediately offered to lend me his extra truck until I could find something permanent. Craig's truck had an extended bed and was incredibly difficult to maneuver, but I was so grateful that I wouldn't have cared if it was lime green.

The Saturday after my return from Colorado, Craig called and asked me to lunch. I told him I needed to look for a car. "Well, let's do lunch first," he said. I conceded.

Over lunch, Craig explained that he planned to buy me a new car (well, a car that was new to me). "Two-thirds will be a Christmas present, and you can repay the remaining one-third at some point in the future," he said. After our meal, he took me car shopping. When it was time to handle payment, he left me out of it. I could just imagine what was going through the salesman's mind. It was probably something like, "This girl's got herself a nice sugar-daddy." But I convinced myself that my embarrassment didn't matter; Craig's generosity deserved my focus.

While Craig had the means to help in this way, his wallet was not overflowing. Said simply, he saw a person in need and decided to help. And he had absolutely no expectation of anything in return for such a massive gift. He even continued getting massages and insisted on paying for them.

Soon after I got the keys to my new Jeep Liberty, I found myself thinking about the moment my truck was towed away. While I did not know *how* I would "rebuild" at the time, I came to appreciate and trust in the unseen. In that horrible moment, I thought no one cared, but Craig showed up to help me, and Francesca was there to comfort me after the accident. This terrifying experience had one major silver lining – the understanding that we're never as alone as we think we are and that life has a way of working itself out.

Like the fellow praying to God to save him from the flood and refusing help from the Jeep, boat and helicopter, we often refuse to accept help when we need it. Craig is a hero, not for giving me a Jeep, but for teach-

try this:

Who are your companions on your journey? Journal about how their talents and gifts contribute to your own life and the world. Seek to find out about the quests they are on.

ing me this lesson. The hero's journey is never undertaken alone. We must recognize the heroes and helpers in others and learn to ask for help if we are to survive and thrive on our quest. The vast majority of people don't like to ask for help, or accept it, even when it could benefit them and those around them greatly. But which would you rather have – your pride or your friends? For me, it's no contest. My friends are much better company.

PRINCIPAL WISER

In my journey of self-discovery, the unveiling has often revealed stubborn and awkward parts of my personality. Many of my life's heroes have been the people who stood by me when I was most difficult to handle. These heroes exercised patience and continued to believe in me, even when I put them through the wringer, so to speak. Their grace, courage and acceptance molded some of my roughest edges.

One such hero was my high school principal. True to his name, Mr. Wiser regularly went to bat for me – a boisterous, sometimes-obnoxious teen – at a time when I often felt the world was against me. I was a handful, but he always offered compassion and encouragement, and defended me from my detractors, taking up a cause few would have cared (or dared) to touch. I liked the image of me I saw mirrored in his eyes, and that made me want to work hard, accomplish amazing feats and shine. Without him, high school could have been a disaster for me rather than the self-confidence turning point it turned out to be.

It wasn't just his confidence in me or his fierce kindness that made such a huge impact; he also offered protection when I felt powerless. During my senior year of high school, Coach Jack, the head track and field coach, had it out for me. At the end of the previous school year, my shot put and discus coach, Coach Paul, retired. So Coach Jack asked a teacher and golf coach, who knew nothing about the sport, to head up my event. This infuriated me. I was a returning state champion and a fierce competitor; I needed a *real* coach.

Yes, I was a bit cocky, but I was one of the top athletes and knew much more about the sport than our new leader. I had just lost the coach who'd brought me to every state track meet since I was a freshman and stood by my side when I won the previous year. He even came to our home to provide extra coaching on the weekends. Coach Paul really cared, and I trusted him, which is not something I did easily. Sports were all I knew to gain the much-needed attention I was getting, and I was terrified this new coach would ruin it for me. So, I thought if I kept practicing the way my former, more talented coach taught me, I'd continue being successful. If the new coach told me to do anything different, I would simply refuse. It was disrespectful, I know, but I was terrified they would ruin my success. The coaches didn't seem to care what I wanted, so I didn't trust them.

Coach Jack didn't appreciate my attitude and gave me a lot of flack during practice – often threatening to throw me off the team. Whenever he made such threats, I called my mother. "Mom, Coach is threatening to kick me off the team again. What do I do?"

"Show up for practice and do your thing, Misti," she would say. Unbeknownst to me, she would then pick up the phone and call Principal Wiser to keep him in the loop.

One day, as I made my way to the locker rooms to prepare for practice, one of the assistant coaches stopped and escorted me to Coach Jack's office. "Misti, you've caused enough disruption," Coach Jack said. "Hand in your uniform and go home. You're off the team."

It took every ounce of self control I had not to punch him in the face. Didn't he know how important athletics were to me? Didn't he understand that I brought back more first-place victories than anyone else on the team? I argued with him for a few minutes and finally walked out. I went directly to Principal Wiser's office. In the midst of my sobbing, Mr. Wiser said, "You're still on the team." While he remained outwardly calm, I could sense his anger. He got up, asked me to stay there and walked out of the office. Of course, I followed him.

Coach Jack was making his way to the track from the gymnasium when Principal Wiser got his attention, pulled him away from the other students and coaches, and said, "If anyone is off this team, it's you." I didn't want them to see me, so I listened only long enough to gain a sense of what was happening. Then, I ran back to Principal Wiser's office and called Mom. Mr. Wiser came back and reassured me and my angry mother, who'd left work immediately and made the 30-minute drive from her office to the school, that I was still on the team.

With a renewed feeling of support, I headed back to practice. Coach Jack didn't say anything more to me. In fact, after that incident, he mostly behaved as if I wasn't even there, which was fine with me. Fearing him took my attention off my great love – shot put and discus. Now, I could focus. That year, I brought back two state championships, won every meet I competed in and broke many records, including my own school record, which I originally set in my sophomore year.

Principal Wiser knew my behavior was not always up to par, and I was certainly not above the law. Mr. Spraggon, our assistant principal, was in charge of disciplining students. Principal Wiser never undermined that authority when I was out of line. Mr. Spraggon once suspended me for fighting, and if I disrespected a teacher or caused problems, I had to spend an hour after school in silence just like the other kids. But Principal Wiser also knew that I needed someone to believe in me and stand by me, even if that meant throwing one of his own coaches off the team. He didn't seem to see things as "right" vs. "wrong;" rather, he was always looking at the bigger picture. And that bigger picture included a reflection of me as a champion, someone worth standing up for, someone who could put up a good fight, someone who could win. And with the vision of his bigger picture in mind, I did win. I continue to remember Principal Wiser as a source of strength and inspiration – as a hero.

DANNY: THE GIFT OF GRACE

❧

Some of my struggles with identity, particularly with unveiling and revealing my sexuality, hurt other people – some who only wanted to help me. In college, as I was just beginning to learn who I was, I was fortunate enough to meet some wonderful people who supported me through the process. Their kindness, even when I wasn't always kind to them, provided me with an incredible foundation to discover and appreciate a part of me I had rejected. One person, in particular, showed me love, even when I was judgmental of him.

A couple months into my freshman psychology class, the professor announced that our next class was optional because of its subject matter. A panel of homosexual members from the community would be discussing their lives and culture. She was pretty much saying, "We're having some gay folks come in to talk about their experience as homosexuals. They might rub off, so attend at your own risk." But I knew this was a class *I* would not miss!

Growing up, the signs had always been there. I was only interested in friendship with boys, nothing more. And when fake-kissing my female playmates, I always wished we didn't have to put our hands between our lips. It wasn't until I started college that I began struggling to embrace what my subconscious had known for some time – I liked girls.

During the panel discussion, my heart raced with concern that one of them might look at me, use her super-sensitive gaydar to identify my embarrassing secret and shout out to the class, "She's one of us!" But despite my fear of being outed, I also was incredibly excited to see a diverse group of women on the panel. Much like my mother, I had always envisioned gay women to look like men, but that wasn't the case with this group. There was one very attractive woman on the panel, who, of course, made my heart (and hormones) race even more. That class settled the whole matter for me. I was definitely gay.

After class, I met the president of the Gay, Lesbian, Bisexual, Transgendered student resource center. A few days later, I got up the guts to call him and proceeded to hang up several times before asking to speak with my new acquaintance. "I met you just after the panel discussion and I'd really like to talk with you," I explained. "But I don't want anyone to see me with you."

Low blow, I know. But Danny was a cross-dresser and he seemed to understand why I was scared to be seen with him in a small town that had little tolerance for homosexuality, especially with respect to men. He was kind, and without one word to remind me that I should be ashamed of myself (he probably knew I already was), he agreed to meet me at the Taco Bell in the Student Center. Yikes! There would be plenty of people there. But, we needed to meet *somewhere*.

I sat on the bench near Taco Bell, anxiously awaiting his arrival and trying to keep a low profile, hoping no one I knew would come over to chat. And then I saw him walking towards me. With a skirt and beard, he was easy to spot in the crowd. I jumped up, said "hello" and asked if we could quickly make our way to my red Ford Ranger, which was parked just down the hill.

I apologized profusely when we got in my truck, but Danny didn't seem to think apologies were necessary, which put me at ease – sort of. We drove to a small parking lot in a local park that I knew to be fairly abandoned on any given day. We parked, and he started to get out. I panicked. "Is it OK for us to stay in the truck?" I asked. I can imagine he was thinking I was being a little ridiculous, but he went with it anyway.

We sat in my truck for more than an hour, and I explained my thoughts about women and my questions and concerns about my sexuality. He listened mostly, which was exactly what I needed. Occasionally, he shared a bit about his experiences, though he must have sensed my anxiety about hearing his stories, because we spent the vast majority of our time together talking about me.

Then, I dropped him off at the Student Center and headed home, praying no one saw me with him and making a conscious decision to put the whole conversation out of my mind for several months. Afterward, when I saw Danny on campus, I would smile but say very little. I certainly didn't want anyone to know I knew him. That would garner questions I wasn't prepared to answer. While I felt bad about how I treated him, I didn't know what else to do.

Almost a year later, after I came out to my parents and found my place in the gay community, I embraced Danny when I saw him. He responded the same way when I embraced him as he had when I avoided him – with kindness. He seemed to respect my coming-out journey and was simply committed to supporting my authentic spirit. He taught me a valuable lesson about meeting people where they are, and about being comfortable enough in my own skin to not always take things personally, especially when someone is having a complete emotional breakdown. He was there for me, and willing to share his compassion and support, with absolutely no expectations from me and no regard for his own pride. In this way, Danny is a hero.

FRANCESCA: THE SECRET SUPERHERO
IDENTIY OF MY PARTNER

I met Francesca while I was the general manager at the Washington Sports Club in Fairfax, Virginia – a job I held for all of three weeks, mostly because I was bored out of my mind. I followed her around like a puppy for 40 minutes while she did cardio, and she flipped me her business card before she left.

A few weeks later, I reached out and arranged a meeting at a local farmers market. Just before we hung up, she said, "I'll bring my partner, Beth."

In my head, I yelled, "What?! Your *partner?* No!" But I'd enjoyed our conversation and still wanted to be friends, so I said that would be great and brought along my friend, Laura, to even things out. Laura and Beth hit it off and ended up leading the way most of the day, which left time for me and Francesca to chat. I couldn't help but be pulled in by the chemistry we shared. As we walked down the street, our arms seemed to stay connected; when we sat on the steps of a building for a short break, our legs touched, and we kept them there.

A couple weeks later, Francesca came over to fix my computer. The attraction was intense, and as we chatted on my couch, I wanted to kiss her. But she was in a relationship. The next day, while chatting over instant messenger, I decided to get my attraction for her out in the open. I told her I knew there was nothing that could be done with this attraction, but she needed to know; rather, I needed to share. She admitted to being attracted to me as well, and that was the end of the conversation. Soon, she and Beth began couple's therapy, and she and I became closer friends. Then four months later, Beth moved out.

Francesca came to my apartment a couple of days later, and our relationship became physical. It was nice in the moment, but my gut told me something wasn't right. After about a month of this, I had a harsh realization – the timing wasn't good for either of us. In the past, I would have forced the relationship because I was afraid to be alone and she was my only friend. But I knew I needed to end the sexual relationship or risk losing my friend. Francesca was upset and a bit shocked but seemed to understand.

One beautiful morning soon after, I decided to clear my head with some outdoor exercise. I put water in my backpack, grabbed my bike and headed to the high-school track a mile from my apartment. After running stairs, sprinting around the track and doing push-ups, I got back on my bike and headed home. Suddenly, I saw a puddle. I swerved to miss it but went right through it. Not wanting to get wet, I grabbed the brakes to slow down – a little too hard. Next thing I knew, the handle bars were beneath me as plowed toward the ground. Thankfully, my left arm cushioned the blow for my head. (Lesson learned: I now wear a helmet.) People came rushing out to help, but I had no insurance and was terrified someone would call an ambulance. I yelled at them to get away and sat alone on the curb.

Through my blurred vision, I called Francesca. She lived 40 minutes away but she was prepared to head my way immediately. "No, no, I'm fine," I said, insisting she wait until I got my senses back and could determine whether she needed to come. I sat for a few more minutes, but my vision didn't clear quickly, and I wanted to get home. I got back on the bike, like a drunken idiot, and peddled my way home. When I got there, I called Francesca, who was already on her way. Once I calmed down, she went back to work.

Francesca and I started sharing more time together. While we were only friends, we acted more like we were dating – giving foot rubs, hugging a lot and sharing our lives. The only thing missing was kissing and sex. One day, she asked me to go for a walk. We made our way through the neighborhoods of Bethesda and found a resting spot against the fence that lines the premises of the National Institutes of Health. "I'm done with this gray zone," she said. "We either need to move forward into a relationship or take some time apart and figure out how to be just friends."

The timing still didn't feel right, so I said, "I guess we'll need to figure out how to be friends. How much time do we need to take from each other?" She never answered that question – or enforced her ultimatum – which made me often think, "All of this and she's still hanging around? She must really like me. I like her too. What's my deal?"

A few weeks later, the holiday season began, and I asked Francesca for a ride to the airport. It was raining, and as I drove to her house, I had a pretty scary accident (the one I described a few chapters back). Instead of doing the sane thing (i.e., calling 911), I called Francesca, who got there as soon as humanly possible and was shaking more than me. The whole time I was in Colorado for Thanksgiving, we spoke at least a couple of times a day. She did her best to comfort me as I cried out of pain and fear, listening as long as I needed her.

I was beginning to see a pattern. I had refused to date her; yet, she was the one always there for me. In fact, she treated me better than any girlfriend I'd ever had – or friend, for that matter.

The day after my return, I went to her house for dinner. She had a bottle of red wine (my favorite) and a beautifully-prepared meal. We ate, chatted, finished the first bottle of wine and began drinking a second bottle – and topped the night off with passionate love making. I went home that night feeling terrible about what I had allowed to happen. I was confused and sending her mixed messages, and she'd been such a good friend to me.

When I called her at work the next day, she answered the phone with a smile in her voice. "It doesn't mean anything, Francesca," I said.

"You're right, it doesn't," she said. I was baffled. She didn't *care* that it didn't mean anything? In reality, she had just figured out how I worked and knew she had me. For the following few months, I demanded that we keep our relationship a secret. I know, I'm usually an over-sharer, but I wanted to be certain it was going to work out before we started telling people. Her response? "You can tell your friends what you want, and I'll tell mine what I want." Her confidence was sexy.

try this:

Journal on an ordinary person in your life and describe how he/she is a hero. Write a tribute and consider sharing it with that person.

This is not where I write, "And they lived happily ever after." As in any relationship, we spent the next few years getting to know each other, and that always means drama – especially because we are so different. Francesca tends to sit with her emotions, while I'm loud and expressive. But thanks to our deep love for each other (and hours of therapy) we *are* happy.

On September 13, 2009, we married. I'm sharing my life with her, because she is the most kind, loving, supportive, nurturing, understanding, open and gentle person I have ever known. My taking time to focus on this book and neglecting to bring in new business means the burden of our bills have rested on her shoulders. But she doesn't see it that way. "Misti, you know how to make money," she told me. "Right now, you're learning how to live your dreams. Stay focused on that and the money will follow." Every day, she helps me to see that we are a team in life; money is only one part of the game, and happiness is our ultimate goal. Francesca is a beautiful mirror – and a hero.

interlude
"RELEASING MY PRISONER"

My breath moves fearlessly through my body
as I claim my inner calmness
shedding my fears of who I should be –
accepting what is and releasing worry of "not enough."

There is no "should" in this moment – there is just me.

These thoughts create a sense of freedom
to do what's closest to my heart
to release that which holds me prisoner.

I embrace this feeling of freedom,
knowing the choice will always reappear.

ONGOING TRANSFORMATION:
Manifesting the Hero Within

One of the most famous heroes of legend, the sea-tossed and ship-wrecked Odysseus had to battle wind, rapids and waves on his epic journey. He clung to his quest and arrived home after many adventures to conquer new challenges and finally find peace with his wife and son. His self confidence and cunning were his most effective weapons, though he could (and would) fight when necessary. Though I have never had to slay a one-eyed giant, outsmart a goddess or fight a hundred men at once, I identify with his resilience. I've discovered that daily disappointments and struggles often offer monumental opportunities to manifest the strong hero within, and to bring out the hero in others.

FINDING CALM
IN THE STORM

Life is often compared to a river, with twists and turns, calm water and intense rapids. The magic is in the way the rough rapids crash against the riverbed and reshape the water's path. Over time, the river changes course but continues to flow. Stop the river? Impossible! Try to slow it by putting up a dam, and the water will eventually erode it away. The water *will* find its way to freedom.

To fight life, to stress about change and go against it, is akin to putting up a dam that will not hold. Just as Mother Nature is carving our beautiful rivers, she is also modeling us. Stop the modeling? Resist the modeling? Why? It's a natural part of our process. It is in these moments that we most need to hang on, stay in our boats, feel alive while the rapids crash against us and remember to notice the beauty, even in the most trying times. Then, we can appreciate the unexpected good that often comes with the changes we fight the hardest.

The waters are not always rough; sometimes they are slow and smooth. But how can we appreciate the peace that follows the rapids if we're stuck under an upturned boat when they arrive? I've never known a time that has felt smooth. In this moment looking back, I can see that calm waters *have* existed at times in my life, but even those *felt* like rapids, and so I resisted, claiming my fear and neglecting my peace.

In the midst of change, my fear wants to take over. But I have a choice – to embrace my fear or trust in my peace. In theory, my calming thoughts feel good; in practice, they are challenging. When I choose to fight the reality of what is, I feel exhausted, as if I have been swimming upstream. While I can steer my boat, and use my skills and experiences to navigate my journey, the river will ultimately take me where it must. I have no control over that. I must learn to just enjoy the ride and allow the current of life, the *experience* of life, to guide and mold me.

To do so, I must trust myself and learn from all the experiences that come my way. And I must keep my eyes and heart open to the adventures, and trust that I will continue to grow. My theory is great; my practice will deliver the woman in the mirror.

Today is the only day I can be sure I have left on this Earth. There are decisions to make in this day, and I will make them from a place of confidence and calmness. The sharp rocks won't be a problem, because I'm choosing to trust in the sturdy craftsmanship of my boat and to enjoy watching the beautiful mountains erode to make way for my growing spirit.

WHOLENESS IS A BALANCING ACT:
HERO WITH TWO FACES

⚜

"We usually look outside of ourselves for heroes and teachers. It has not occurred to most people that they may already be the role model they seek ... our wholeness exists in us now ... it can be remembered."

RACHEL NAOMI REMEN, *KITCHEN TABLE WISDOM*

This spirit of mine (perhaps the true spirit in all of us) is made up of two powerful forces, which are in constant relationship with each other – sometimes antagonistic, sometimes harmonious, sometimes one in the same. But neither of them is any good without the other.

My understanding of this inner relationship has evolved over time and experience. Before beginning the journey that has become this book, I considered my adult self the core of who I really am, minus all my reactions and fears. I envisioned my adult self as the one who is heroic, calm and self-possessed, who lives in the present moment and, therefore, comes from a place of love and trust. Wouldn't everyone want a hero like her?

I saw my little girl as a brat who needed pampering and saving. Where my adult self was present and strong, my little girl was weak, stuck in the past and worried about the future. Whenever she felt unsafe and started pitching a temper tantrum, my adult self would have to swoop down, assuage my little girl's fears and avert the emotional crisis of the moment. I saw the two as opposites, who were often at war, and I was stuck mediating between the hero and the needy little pest – wasting precious time and energy and never feeling completely balanced.

As the journey chronicled and this book unfolded, the layers that kept these two from understanding one another's intentions and value fell away. I know now that the hero within, my soul and my strength, is not embodied in my adult self alone. It is, in fact, made up of both of them, equal parts child and adult, and they take turns creating peace and rescuing one another.

My inner child may express herself in a way that is, well … childish. But she has great maturity, wisdom and instincts at her core. Her kicking and screaming has alerted my adult self to pay close attention and thus saved me from danger many times – when I'm ignoring some emotion or memory that I should be addressing and even when I'm in physical danger.

While walking toward the D.C. metro station late one Saturday evening seven years ago, I suddenly found myself unable to move forward. Shannon, my girlfriend at the time, was annoyed with the delay. "Come on, Misti, let's go," she insisted.

"I can't move, Shannon," I said with a bit of irritation in my tone. I looked down the street to my left and spotted a crowd of people walking towards the metro station. We quickly joined their larger (and therefore safer) group. Approximately 20 feet in front of the spot where I'd frozen, I saw three men come out of a stairwell. While I cannot guarantee they were going to mug us that night, my gut told me we escaped a very bad situation. The stubborn little girl in me refused to cooperate. My intuition – that strange, "irrational" gut feeling – took over, because deep down, the little girl knew better than the adult in that critical moment.

As a child, I was often wild, annoying, obnoxious, needy, loud, demanding and deceitful – and so is the little girl who still thrives inside of me today. It was by the strength of who I was as a child that I survived. I was brutally honest, leading those who knew me well to the conclusion that the filter between my brain and mouth was damaged. I still speak my truth, though in the grown-up world, where white lies are expected in the name of politeness, my tendency to tell the whole truth often leaves me with my size-nine feet stuck in my big mouth. While it often got me in trouble, I never just assumed someone with authority was right; my curiosity and demanding nature led me to question everything and thereby gain a deeper understanding about the "why's" in life. I love this quality in me today.

My closest friends remind me that my curiosity was supposed to dwindle at age 2. Not this girl; cats have nothing on me.

I was also deeply loving, daring and fun. I love that I was (and, thanks to my two-dimensional hero, still am) always willing to take risk for the sake of the thrill and, let's face it, to impress others. Today, I use this same quality for the same reasons. During a recent walk with my intern, I stopped a little boy on a three-wheeler. "Excuse me, young man," I said. "Can I ride?" My intern looked at me like I was crazy, not believing I would actually try to ride the tiny contraption. The boy agreed to share. I forced my way into the seat and tried to push the pedals, with no success. I thanked the little boy and walked away laughing with my intern. I love that my little girl keeps me spontaneous, wild and passionate – about work and play.

Thankfully, my adult self and little girl have gotten better at judging who should take the reins in a given situation. On the subject of passion in my work, a mentor once told me, "Misti, think of your passion as a tool in your tool belt. If you're hanging a picture, would you use a sledge hammer or a small hammer?"

"A small hammer, of course," I replied.

"Use that same principle when interacting with others at networking functions," she said. "If you go around spewing your passion everywhere, you're going to scare many people away. Use it when you *need* it."

So, I have to give my little girl her "playtime" when I can. That way, when I'm at a networking function, she doesn't jump out and scare people. But I trust that while she may not filter herself, she always knows what's up, and if she sounds an alarm, digs in her heels, or flares up in anger, she is alerting my adult self to a danger or an important truth. When she doesn't allow me to rest peacefully, I know I'm missing something and need to pay attention.

Sometimes, she rears up at inopportune moments, and I have to trust my adult self to deal with her fears while remaining calm. The balance is often tenuous at best. This is especially true when I'm not alone, or worse, on stage. While I've been facilitating panels and workshops for years, I have only recently begun my foray into keynote speaking. And I landed the biggest speaking gig of my career thus far when NASA asked me to address 1,200 of its highest-ranking technology leaders.

I spent months preparing for this speech and I felt good about it. Unfortunately, my little girl got stage fright. Although the speech was not a total disaster, I had trouble controlling my nerves and my emotions. It was as if I let the little girl take over on stage, and all she could do was clutch her teddy bear and forget our lines.

The speech started off strong. Then, I forgot where I was, which led to a thunderous wave of self-beatings, making it impossible to get back on track. Notes? Yeah, I looked at them several times, but they were useless without confidence. When I got to the part in my speech about Socrates and self-knowledge, something I'm truly passionate about, I was able regain a touch of trust that I knew what I was doing. And I finished strong.

But it was too late. I felt that I had already failed. As I went back to my seat, I was sure I'd messed up the biggest opportunity of my career and probably lost all credibility in the business community. A wave of emotion hit me – fear, disappointment, embarrassment, frustration. The tears began to form in my eyes. As if I needed anything else to feel mortified about on that stage. "Deep breaths, Misti," my adult self told us. Didn't work. Time to get creative. "Focus on this Tic Tac, Misti," she said, trying to help me pull it together. "Put it in your mouth and just focus on it, nothing else." Crunch, crunch. It helped. I had another.

I know it sounds crazy, but those tiny orange candies helped me pull it together. Hey, whatever works, right? Off I went to sign books, tear-free but still berating myself a little. "They're not going to want my book," I thought, swallowing hard. I kept the tears at bay as people greeted me on my way out the door.

A few people were waiting at my signing table, including a gentleman who felt it appropriate to share his thoughts about my speech. "You lost your shit, Misti," he said.

Rather than drop-kick his ass, which was, I admit, my initial instinct, my adult self went into protective mode. "No, I didn't lose my shit," I said calmly. "I forgot my place several times and I was exceptionally nervous. Have a good day."

I was also met by many kind people who somehow didn't notice my nervousness on stage, or were at least a little more forgiving of my imperfection. They appreciated the long, dramatic pauses and didn't mind that I looked at my notes. They shared kind words of appreciation and let me know what they took away from my speech, which helped tremendously. Some even gave me a hug. Whew! My career wasn't over.

Later, my therapist Samantha asked, "Misti, would you bring a seven year old on stage with you to a speech like that? You have work to do out there, and sometimes it makes sense to bring your little girl. Other times, it does not, and you need to leave her in your hotel room with a teddy bear and let her know you'll celebrate with her upon your return."

Striking the right balance between my nervous little girl and my confident adult self is a never-ending practice. Ignoring either leads me into trouble. But when they are given equal value and attention, life seems to work out. The two must trust one another and learn to work and play together on this, my journey.

Together, they have learned (and are still perfecting) the balancing act between dealing with the hurts of the past and anxiety about the future, and being present in today. Embracing the not-knowing is frightening; yet, it is in that space I have gathered the richness within these pages and within my life. I now understand what the brilliant Zig Ziglar meant when he wrote, "It's when you're in the valley that you grow the crops that you eat when you're on the mountain top."

My life has proven there are many brilliant overlooks where the view is great, but no mountain top. Thinking in this way frees me to enjoy each step of the journey, without needing to know what comes next.

I began this book in the exact spot I'm now sitting – on a chair, at the end of a long dining room table, in an old but well-kept home, owned by a woman who hardly knows me yet generously shares with me. A year ago, I came to this house in a small town called Lewes, Delaware, to finish a book I had already begun on young professionals in the workplace. But when I began typing, what appeared on the computer screen had nothing to do with intergenerational dynamics and careers. After finding myself completely unsuccessful at keeping myself on topic, and with no understanding of what was to come, I allowed my writing to go where it chose. While I truly thought this book was going to become a redefinition of the idea of heroism, I came, instead, to discover the hero within me.

Of course, many other heroes have played a role in my journey, and each of them managed to lead me back to myself. I borrowed their belief in me until I could find it in myself. Reliving my story and remembering each of these extraordinary people has reminded me that I am not alone.

My journey has taught me to look deep beneath the layers and into the core of myself and others to see beyond what's seemingly irritating or "wrong" and focus instead on the beauty, kindness, gifts and mirrors they provide.

I've also learned that, thanks to the layers of self-protection we create, it's not always easy to see ourselves clearly. But the people around me show me a reflection of my core self and help me unearth the parts of myself hidden deep beneath the ground in mines so dangerous and unsteady that even coal miners would hesitate to go searching around. Terrified to get into the rickety elevator that would take me underground, where I could be buried alive by my pain and insecurity, I gathered my courage, took a deep breath and went anyway. Finding trust within ourselves will ultimately free us from any worry of such a disaster. And if the disaster should surface, that trust in our instincts and our own strength will keep us safe.

This process begins with oneself and graciously permeates the world around us. The more kindness and peace we find within, the more we have to offer. Just as this journey has led me to fall in love with many aspects of myself, including those I once considered dark, bad or wrong, and my hope is that you, too, will redefine your stories, rediscover and unveil the parts of yourself you have rejected, and fall completely in love with who you are – all of you.

NOTES

NOTES

acknowledgements

I don't know if this book would have ever come to be without the support of Taylor Mallory, my initial guiding editor. In addition to being one of the best editors I know, Taylor has become a sister. As I struggled through the emotions associated with some of the stories in this book and needed someone to talk to, she was there. She listened patiently and offered some of the most kind and reassuring words I could hope to hear. Thank you for all you are, Taylor!

The structure and flow of this book would not be what it is without the support of Leslee Johnson, a woman who has taught me a great deal about trusting in oneself and the importance/excitement of continued learning. Thank you, Leslee, for taking a stand for and believing in this book, even when I lost sight of its magic.

Jennifer Tyson is the brilliant woman responsible for the design and layout of the book. More than a creative genius, she is a kind woman, an exceptional mom and a loving friend. Thank you, Jennifer!

A critical component to the success of any book is marketing. If no one knows about it, it doesn't matter how great it is; people won't read it. The following are the women (and gentleman) who served as reviewers for my book and/or on my advisory committee for the book launch: Kristina Bouweiri, Vannessa Calderon, Cynthia De Lorenzi, Kelly Harman, DeAnn Malone, Yvette Nash, Mali Phonpadith, Steven Thomas, Linda Cureton and Kim Russo. Thank you taking the time to provide your valuable insight and for supporting me in all that I do.

Finally, I would like to thank Vernice Armour, Sam Horn, Edie Fraser and Julie Kantor for being incredible role models and selfless supporters of others' dreams — mine included! Thank you!